# THE LONG ROAD HOME

She had known for a long time that something was the matter with Peter. But what does a wife do when her husband refuses to communicate and shuts her out? What does she do when her worst fears come true? What does she say to their three teenage children and an enquiring three-year old?

This is a wife's story, the deeply-moving record of Peter's last year – and the year that followed. It is full of pain. Yet it touches the heart with warmth. Peter's road home in the end brings healing, perfect, complete. For Wendy the long road continues. With agonizing slowness she leaves behind the valley of shadows, helped by faith and small but certain miracles.

'Let there be new beginnings,' Peter said. A year after his death that almost seems possible.

Wendy Green lives in east London. She is a trained teacher and was married to her primary school headmaster husband, Peter, for eighteen years until his sudden death from cancer.

She has a teenage son and daughter, David and Margaret, an adopted daughter, Debra, also in her teens, and Jenny, a little girl of six, born when Wendy was in her mid-thirties. In addition to running a home and bringing up a lively family, Wendy has written a number of books for both children and adults.

# THE LONG
# ROAD HOME

WENDY GREEN

A LION PAPERBACK
Tring · Belleville · Sydney

Copyright © 1985 Wendy Green

Published by
**Lion Publishing plc**
Icknield Way, Tring, Herts, England
ISBN 0 7459 1107 2
**Lion Publishing Corporation**
10885 Textile Road, Belleville, Michigan 48111, USA
ISBN 0 7459 1107 2
**Albatross Books Pty Ltd**
PO Box 320, Sutherland, NSW 2232, Australia
ISBN 0 86760 811 0

First edition 1985
Paperback edition 1986

**Acknowledgments**
Bible quotations are from the Authorized King James
Version, the *Jerusalem Bible* © 1966 by Darton, Longman
and Todd Ltd and Doubleday and Company, Inc., and
*The Good News Bible* © 1966, 1971 and 1976 American
Bible Society, published by Bible Societies/Collins.
'When I think of thy heavens' © Ewald Bash is from
*Youth Praise 2*, published by Falcon/Kingsway.
The Cliff Richard song, 'It has to be me, it has
to be you', by Paul Field and Dave Cooke is
quoted with permission of the copyright
owners, Waif Music, ATV Music Limited,
19 Upper Brook St, London.

Cover photograph: ZEFA

**British Library Cataloguing in Publication Data**
Green, Wendy
    The long road home.
    1. Bereavement——Psychological aspects   2. Cancer
    ——Patients   3. Adjustment (Psychology)
    I. Title
    306.8'8     BF575.G7
    ISBN 0 7459 1107 2

Printed in Great Britain
by Cox and Wyman, Reading

PART ONE

# Valley of the Shadow

SOMETHING IS THE MATTER WITH PETER. I can't reach through to him any more. His eyes avoid me. He is restless, tense . . . with a tension that is more than his usual boundless nervous energy that overflows into involvement with all the causes that mean so much to him . . . the primary school where he is headmaster, the education authority, the summer holiday mission he runs each year at Nefyn on the north-west tip of Wales, the local church, our multi-racial community.

He has lost half a stone in weight and two inches round the waist — but he won't go to the doctor's, or if he does he comes back with a bottle of white indigestion mixture and a roll of tablets.

He spends hours on the telephone, or talking to other people, but if I want to talk about family matters he says he is tired, or has enough worries. I am beginning to wonder if I am superfluous to requirements, except for such practical trivia as clean shirts and socks, and the best way of relieving tense nervous energy.

If I try to pursue the matter, get through to the root of his preoccupation he pushes me away: I don't think he realizes it but sometimes his hands actually lift in a pushing movement, palms towards me, at arms length.

'Go away,' they say. 'Don't come near me. This is my space. I don't want you invading it.'

I retreat, hurt, to lick my wounds.

I spend hours worrying, analyzing, asking myself where I have gone wrong. Am I too demanding, too possessive? Have I been too wrapped up in the children and my work? Am I neurotic, as he implies? Yes. There has to be an element of truth in all those accusations. I can be no easier a person to live with than he is. We are both only children, both used to having things our own way, and both imperfect. It has made for an interesting eighteen years of marriage.

Now, for the first time ever, I begin to wonder what the next eighteen will hold. If there will be another eighteen, even. Is this just a temporary setback — the kind of hiccup that disturbs all close relationships, sporadically? Or is it some fundamental flaw at the root of the relationship which is going to require more drastic treatment? Whatever it is, I am digging my heels in, fretting at the problem like a terrier worrying a rabbit. Too much is at stake to ignore it — even if Peter would let me. When I do try to subdue my over-active imaginings, he usually manages to stir them into fresh action with some casual word or action.

I have to talk to people about marriage as part of my work.

'What do you see as the good things about marriage?' I enquire.

The answers hardly vary.

'Friendship, companionship, the best friend I ever had.'

It is like salt in an open wound. We are not companions, 'helpmeets' as the oldest story in the Book describes it; not at the moment anyway. There is a great divide between us. I don't understand what is going on in him and he doesn't appear to want to know what is going on in me. It is a thin wedge, which is widening into an almighty chasm. The prospect of dropping into the abyss is terrifying.

☆      ☆

I go to the library and pore through books on male menopause, mid-life crisis, the 'funny forties'. They assure me it is a 'temporary phase' which he will grow out of in six to ten years. I would see the funny side of it, if it wasn't so serious. Some days I wonder if we will survive the next six weeks.

I listen to other women discussing their partners' faults and foibles: the frustrations simmering never far beneath the surface in a relationship as close and demanding as marriage. I am reassured to know we are not abnormal, that I am no more neurotic than the next person. What I don't know is how to start working towards a solution to this present impasse.

If only we could talk. Properly. Not just about West Ham's chances for the Cup, or who said what at County Hall, or selection procedures for secondary education, or whether a road should be moved six inches to the left or right. These things may be important. They can also be very effective diversionary tactics.

One day I ask him what he wants of me. He replies, 'Just to be there.'

I am not impressed. The furniture is 'just there' too. That is used, sometimes abused, and needs to be replaced every seven to ten years. I have no intention of sharing a similar fate.

He says he is no good at saying what he thinks about things. I say he doesn't want to think — at least, not about the things I'm pressing him about. I make a supreme effort, after years of suppressing my thoughts and feelings, and try to put some of my anxieties into words. I await the comeback apprehensively, but there is none. It's as if the sentences have slid past him and disappeared into space, leaving me even more hollow, and empty, and shut up inside myself.

He stands at the front of the church in his lay reader's robes, alone, cut off from the congregation, lost in thought. We are supposed to be singing a worship hymn.

'I want to reach out and touch him, and tell him I love him,' chorus the rest of the congregation. The tears stream down my face. I know the words are not intended to refer to a human relationship but they sum up so much of how I feel about Peter. But how can I convey it? I am not good at expressing my emotions, or even acknowledging that I have any. Now I feel shut out, excluded. I think he feels judged, pushed into a corner. The dangers are obvious but he refuses to see them.

'I'm OK,' he says. 'There's nothing the matter. It's all in your mind.'

I only wish it were.

☆       ☆

I almost need to keep pinching myself to see if it is true. We are camping in a field of buttercups at the foot of a hill fort in the Welsh border country. Alone. The children are with my mother. London, home, is a hundred and fifty miles away. The sun is hot. The sky is cloudless. The only sounds are the bleating of sheep, a distant skylark, the occasional mournful call of a cow, and the babble of the brook where we splash and shiver when we have had enough of the sun.

We can read, relax, be. There are no demands, no people. It's like being halfway to heaven. Or nearer. Shropshire is my spiritual homeland. I was formed here, spent the formative years of my life amongst snowdrops and primroses, cowslips and rose hips. We fetched our drinking-water in billy cans from a spring half a mile away, entertainment was a walk through the woods or over-grown lanes, civilization the weekly trip to Ludlow on market day. Since then trees and woods and water and semi-wildness have always had power to soothe my city-shattered nerves, speak peace to my soul.

Even Peter is unwinding, after a false start. We had hardly manoeuvred the caravan through the usual im-possible entrance before he was back on the road, head in the engine of a car which had spluttered to an undignified halt. Within seconds he had diagnosed lack of petrol, syphoned some from our tank, and the young driver and his wife were on their way rejoicing.

To see him at last sitting still, taking his time over his food, enjoying the tranquillity as much as I am, is nothing short of miraculous. Put him within five yards of people and he must be organizing, agitating, mobilizing them. I gave up trying to keep pace with him years ago. It has always been a source of exasperation to us both. He finds my 'share it with someone else wherever possible' philos-ophy more than frustrating. I fret that he will burn himself out, long before the allotted three-score years and ten.

Even here he cannot stay put for more than a couple of hours. We must be consulting maps, timetables, guide books, plotting out the days. Not for nothing did the teachers in his school in Dorset nickname school journeys 'Pete's lightning tours'.

We travel on the mid-Wales railway to Llandrindod Wells. He is like a boy again, touring the country, train-spotting with his mates. It is good to see him so enthusiastic, free from the responsibilities of committees and education, spiritual and political warfare in high places.

A sudden thunderstorm leaves me with a soaking skirt. I

strip it off, and walk the main street of the Welsh spa town with gangling legs and knobbly knees protruding beneath my brief shorts and long kagool. It is not a pretty sight, but Pete seems to think it is hilarious. He spots an advert for a trip on the post bus around the reservoirs which supply Birmingham with water. Our tickets are postage stamps. I almost expect the post office clerk to slap them on my damp posterior, but he thinks better of it and provides us with an official card.

We take our seats alongside farmers rather the worse for wear after a morning in the market, telling ribald jokes despite the disapproving frowns of their robust wives. I don't know who is more amused: them, at the strangers mad enough to spend four hours in a dormobile doing a tour of outlying Welsh post offices, or us, getting a glimpse into a world so different from the pseudo-sophistication of the capital city. Halfway round, the postman/driver pauses at a garage-cum-tearoom, does a quick count of heads and signals seven to the man at the pumps. On our return trip from the village, seven cups of tea are waiting, once we have braved the gaggle of geese who have appointed themselves guardians of this particular outpost.

The next day we take a walk along an older line of defence, Offa's Dyke. I am in my element, fulfilling a lifelong ambition, spinning plans of how one day it would be good to walk much further, dispensing with cars and caravans and all the modern limits to mobility. I feel myself back into the minds of those who warred over these in-between, border territories, identify with their struggles. I am no stranger to conflict between rival factions, though the battles I fight are those common to flesh and spirit trying to co-exist in the latter half of the twentieth century.

I wonder if Peter is experiencing similar feelings, but do not have the courage to ask. It could be too close for comfort. I have had one go at expressing my anxieties and got him so wound up that all the healing of the past three days came rapidly undone. He needs this space to recharge his batteries. They are at a low enough ebb already. Heaven only knows how he will cope with the final six weeks of the summer term, to say nothing of running a three-week holiday mission directly afterwards. At the moment it looks as if he could hardly limp to the bottom of this hill. I try to re-energize him with chocolate biscuits and mints. It works — to a limited extent. But he is still not really with me. Some part of him is far away, I do not want to know where. I shake the thought away. Peter rouses himself, tries to brush aside the questions in my eyes with a joke. I can't help feeling he is trying to put on a superb act especially for my benefit. It's as if he knows I am worrying about him, and he is doing all in his power to convince me there is no cause for concern. Unfortunately for him he is not a good actor, and I am a born sceptic. I remain unconvinced.

We visit the small Shropshire town of Church Stretton, set amongst the hills. We dam a stream with pebbles and an old car tyre, and sit dangling our feet in the cool water, much to the disquiet of a lone minnow. By the time we have clambered over the summit of the hill and fought our way back down a valley waist-high in bracken, Pete is exhausted. He shrugs it off with some excuse, and a cup of tea and a sticky bun appear to revive him. Ten minutes later he is negotiating the car up a one-in-four incline. There is a terrifying drop to the valley on the scale of a James Bond movie. Thunder reverberates around the hills and the rain bounces from the pebbly surface of the track. Within minutes a torrent is racing us for the valley on the other side of the hill. I have never in all my life felt so exposed to the elements. Peter appears to enjoy pitting his skill against the storm. I thank God for safety belts, and the fact that he is a superb driver.

'Want to take over?' he teases.

I shake my head. How could I deprive him of his moment of glory, or risk the possibility of leaving four orphaned children?

On our last evening we climb to the hill fort. The lane leading up to it is banked with bluebells and wild strawberry flowers. We skirt a field of young wheat, and cross a second, covered in gorse and coarse grass. The view to the heartlands of Wales is spectacular. We are on an outcrop of a plateau, flanked on three sides by valleys. Sheep graze on the earthworks which would once have been such an important refuge and defence. Ditch after ditch rises to a central mound. The scale of the task is mind-blowing. It puts the petty building achievements of the modern world to shame. Skyscrapers may stretch to the stars. Caer Caradoc is one with the sky, the woods, the slow-fading daylight. There is something timeless, elemental about it. For once my two conflicting natures are harmonized. So are Peter and I. It is a blessing Welsh sheep are not easily shocked.

☆     ☆

Summer in London. Dry streets. Dust. Hay fever. Frayed tempers. End of term exhaustion. Only a month to the holiday mission in Nefyn. Phone ringing. Letters. People needing information about transport, accommodation, beach talks, catering. Prayer letters to write. Publicity. Teaching materials.

Peter doesn't want to know. I take whatever burdens I can, and simmer with fury. He should have given this up five years ago. But he wouldn't listen — won't ever listen. Can't bear to admit that he could possibly be wrong — disastrously wrong in some cases.

'Just do as I say,' he instructs, 'and you'll be all right.' I wish I could believe it.

I try to ignore the underlying problem which is adding to the tensions. But a careless word or action can bring it bobbing straight to the surface. Invariably we end up with tears and traumas, and a reluctant truce. Till the next time.

I know the older children must be aware that something is wrong, and try to alleviate their worst fears.

'It's OK,' I say reassuringly. 'I know we're having a lot of arguments, but we're trying to work things through. We have no intention of ending up in the divorce courts.'

'Please, God,' I add, under my breath.

☆     ☆

I sit in a garden in Surrey staring at the woods in the far

distance, while a group of friends discuss the virtue of suffering. I am astounded at the way they seem to regret lacking the experience. Coping with the suffering others have told me about through broken marriages and unemployment is bad enough. No way would I wish it for real, or any more real than it is already.

Three years ago, my cousin lost her husband and little girl in a car accident. In February my father died. Now Peter. Peter? What is going to happen to us?

The sky beyond the woods seems to mushroom, unfold, no longer to set the limit of my horizon. It is like looking through into another world, another dimension. A voice says clearly, authoritatively, 'I will hold you.'

It is not the voice of my friends. They are continuing their conversation, oblivious to what I am experiencing. I am shaken. I am no Joan of Arc, given to hearing voices, receiving divine revelations — especially with all the implications that one contains.

'Go away, God,' I mutter grimly. 'You've got the wrong person. It's this lot who want to make themselves martyrs. Not me.'

I try to forget it. That is not difficult. I have an appalling memory, and there are plenty of things to absorb my attention, with three teenagers, a toddler, and a husband rediscovering his lost adolescence.

I work at the factors which could have contributed to his restlessness, the stress which is manifesting itself in so many physical symptoms.

As an only child myself, I can appreciate the incredibly high expectations we unconsciously absorb. I know how many of my own tensions spring from the continual and irrational feeling of never quite making the grade. When you carry that kind of thinking into your Christian commitment there are going to be problems. If Peter is having to handle emotions that run counter to all he has believed and expected of himself, no wonder he is continuing to lose weight, especially when he finds it so difficult to articulate what he feels.

☆     ☆

'I need to be me,' Peter announces in a rare burst of self-expression.

That comes as a rather startling revelation. I have never thought of him as anything other than a highly flamboyant, very individual, individual. He has always appeared to 'do his own thing', regardless of the petty restrictions of church, state, education authority, or marriage partner. He shows very little fear or favour to any of the powers that be, save the One to whom we are all answerable. If he feels bogged down now, is that coming from the pressure of the family, or all the other commitments he has taken on board over the years?

'Don't try to change him,' warned an older friend when we got engaged.

It would have been pointless trying. He is not one to respond favourably to 'Thou shalt/shalt not'. Besides, I don't think of God as a dictator, bossing his creation around at his pleasure, but as a father who knows us through and through, and gently shows us the paths that are best for us. Should I treat his children with less respect? Even one as confused and confusing, as Peter?

I try to point out possible consequences of various options, make him understand a little of my feelings — when I understand, or will admit them, myself. I cannot, will not, make the choices for him.

Maybe that's where I'm going wrong? Maybe he needs me to take a more positive stance, to rant and rave, insist he should see things my way? Others seem to have no hesitation in pressing their opinions. Will I lose by default because I have always tried to give him the freedom to be himself, to choose?

Lord God, what agonies you must endure watching the liberties we take with your love, and the glorious messes we create for ourselves in the process. I haven't your patience. I don't pretend to have grasped even a glimmer of that perfect love. I am frightened, very frightened. Help me to know when to be understanding, when to dig in my heels. Help me to see beyond my own hurt to whatever is making him like he is, for all our sakes. I can sympathize with the need to establish his own identity. Generations of women have grappled with that problem, affections divided between the demands of their children, their commitment to their partner, and their own need to remain a person. There are no easy answers, though a sorting out of priorities must come pretty near the top of the list.

I ask Peter one day what his priorities are. He replies without hesitation, 'School, Nefyn mission, the church.' When I ask where that leaves the family, he rams his foot so hard on the accelerator I expect to end up in a place where the subject will no longer bother me. Apparently the answer is so obvious, I am an idiot for asking the question. I do not pursue the matter. How can an idiot argue with a headmaster, particularly when he is behind the wheel of a very powerful car?

☆    ☆

Even Nefyn doesn't seem to have a particularly high priority at the moment though, despite the fact that it looms ever nearer. I do what I can to answer people's queries. But there are some days when I feel that far from being the last mission Peter is going to lead, there will be no mission at all. I joke with the children about 'end of term-itis' and the funny forties. We talk about the confusion and conflict they are experiencing, as they move from childhood to adolescence, and how maybe dad is experiencing very similar feelings. It is too much to expect that they will be able to move out much towards him, but hopefully it will reduce the level of their hurt when he is abrupt, or absorbed, or not able to cope with their noise and exuberance.

If only someone could do the same for me . . . release me from the downward spiral of anxiety and self-pity, the overwhelming sense of loss which opens up every time Peter excludes me, pushes me away.

I have one of those dreams where you are desperately trying to get away from someone and everything keeps hindering you, tripping you up, creating new obstacles. I rush into a lift, thinking I have escaped at last, only to find myself shrinking till I am no bigger than a Borrower. Now I am really trapped. I cannot reach the button to open the doors. There is no way out — unless someone else can release me.

I take the point. Peter will not acknowledge that we need help, but I must have some from somewhere, however much it may hurt my pride to admit it. One day, when I am feeling desperate, I phone a long-standing friend with counselling experience, and roll the terrific burden of feeling rejected and unloved along the line. He says I am involved in a holding operation. All I can do is hold on to Peter, and God. I must remember that however I feel, I am loved as a daughter, very special and very precious.

That stops me in my tracks. I can't put the phone down quickly enough. I guess Len has forgotten, or God has prompted him to touch the weak spot in my defences. Loved as a daughter? An only daughter? Extra special and extra precious? Oh dad. Mum and I could do so little for you. We could see your fears about being made re-dundant, your concern about managing financially, your depression when you could not get back to work after the first heart attack. We tried to tell you how much we loved you, to hold on to you. But words are so inadequate, even when we can bring ourselves to use them. Did you understand? How can I make Peter understand how much we love and need him?

I do not cry easily, but I cry now. When the worst flood is over, I open the Bible, my constant source of guidance and strength. But the words which leap out at me do not bring the message of consolation I want to hear. Far from it.

'Do not weep for the man who is dead . . .' they instruct. 'Weep bitterly for the man who has gone away, since he will never come back.'

When I have recovered from the initial shock, I argue with God. 'It's coincidence. You can't possibly mean it.' Logic switches into action. Stop taking it out of context, seeking reassurance at random. It is a dangerous game. 'Has God ever lied, when scripture has spoken as clearly as that?' nags another level of my brain.

'Oh Lord. You don't really mean it, do you? Not Peter? Gone away? For ever?' Even my gloomy forebodings don't have quite such a disastrous outcome. I am crying again, weeping bitterly as instructed. But I am not sure if it is for the man who has gone away, or those he is leaving behind.

☆     ☆

It has happened. We have survived, despite all the indications to the contrary. After a twenty-year commitment, Peter has led the mission at Nefyn for the last time. There will be no more beach talks to prepare, no more feeding of forty hungry team members, no more responsibility for 300 children playing games in and out of cars, boats, irate picnickers and the sea, no more sixteen-hour working days in what is supposed to be Peter's summer break.

Next year, when people ask, 'Where are you going for your holiday?' I shall not have to answer 'Nefyn' — with the mental after-tag, 'What holiday?' If I have any say in the matter we shall be several hundred miles south, relaxing in the sun, instead of huddling behind wind-breaks in our anoraks, or taking part in a beach hockey match with one of the parents yelling, 'Never mind the ball, get their legs,' and the wife of the international director of our parent body ending up with her front tooth knocked out.

The partings have been painful, but we all know they are not permanent. Next year I may get my way but it will be a one-off occasion. We will be back again. Peter and the children will make sure of that. I shall just have to make sure I have a very strong piece of rope to tie him to his deckchair.

☆     ☆

'Isn't it sad,
isn't it strange,
we say we need to rearrange,
Never ourselves,
always somebody else.
Another defence,
another excuse,
pointing the finger where we choose —
Just don't believe it's ourselves we deceive,'

Cliff Richard sings, on the latest tape Peter has bought me.

'It has to be you.

It has to be me.

Everyone together,'

punches the chorus, in case we haven't got the message.

It is a timely reminder. Jesus warned about trying to dislodge the speck of sawdust from your brother's eye when you couldn't see, for the beam in your own. If Pete and I are to get beyond the flashpoints in our relationship we both have plenty of work to do on ourselves. I need to root out the insecurities that make me feel so threatened and inadequate. He is working on the insensitivity that catapults me into a defensive position. Sometimes it works, sometimes it doesn't. But at least we are trying.

We both make a conscious effort to pull back from some of the commitments that make such heavy demands and leave so little time for one another and the children. We should have done it years ago. Now the need is urgent. The older ones are at too crucial an age to let them feel neglected. So are Peter and I. The jokes used to be about the seven-year itch. Now marriage counsellors are becoming seriously concerned about the twenty-year one. We have taken one another for granted too long. It is obviously time for a new initiative.

David and Margaret go to football with him. Saturdays revolve around whether or not West Ham are playing at home. I have visions of them being knifed on the terraces by teenage yobos, but Peter assures me the only violence he has ever seen was when two fifty-year-olds came to blows. They seem to have forgotten the incident when they went to Chelsea and both Peter and David ended up scrambling over someone's garden wall for safety, as the police horses charged a mob hurling insults and bottles.

If West Ham win, they celebrate by bringing home bags of sprats or kippers and the whole house reeks of frying fish. If they lose, we have ten minutes silence while they recover with a cup of strong tea, followed by a post-mortem for the rest of the evening. One night Peter even persuades me to go . . . with the proviso that we have a seat. I have no intention of standing on the terraces for two hours while two dozen grown men kick a ball from one end of the pitch to the other. It is an experience I would not have missed, but am in no hurry to repeat.

In return, I at last manage to convince him that I am not joking when I say the teachers at the children's comprehensive school must think we are a single parent family, he so rarely puts in an appearance at any of the functions. I know it is another pressure at the end of a busy day but 'O' level exams, options, and possible school closures are important. Besides, he's much better than I am at chatting up the female members of staff.

There is another bonus too. The local pub is just across the road. Once the business is over, we can pop in there for an hour's break. There are no telephones, no television, and no teenagers. We can sit and talk, or simply watch a cross-section of our multi-racial community relaxing, relating. This is one of the scenes that never hits the headlines: a twentieth-century inner city community, in a pub used as a hunting-lodge by King Henry VIII. When we have youngsters from out of town staying with us, Peter likes to wind them up by telling them there is a secret passage from the pub to West Ham football stadium, the Boleyn ground, so that Henry could pop out with Ann for a quick pint at half time. The youngsters listen, wide-eyed. People never quite know what to make of Peter on first acquaintance. When he emerges in his lay reader's robes on a Sunday morning they are even more taken aback. They seem to have some difficulty reconciling the laugh-a-minute entertainer with the more serious side of his nature.

He needs freedom to be himself? Which self? The listening ear, the comforter? The administrator who can solve every problem, usually single handed? The handyman, able to fix anything from a camshaft to a cuckoo clock? The whirlwind, the enthusiast, the energizer, who can mobilize a roomful of people with a brusque, 'Come on then. Let's get going.'? (And woe betide them if they are not ready at least half an hour before the scheduled activity.) I sigh. What about the man beneath all that, with hopes, dreams, fears of his own? I may not be very good at helping him articulate them but at least I can manoeuvre him a little space to try.

The children learn to accept that they should not monopolize the lounge and the television the entire evening, that there are times when dad needs to relax with the paper and a tape of his favourite music for half an hour.

We go to the cinema, have meals out, probably spend more time together than at any other phase of our married life. Peter enjoys eating out. He seems to have less problem with his digestion when the pace of the meal is more leisurely. He may not always be able to eat as much as he used to, but neither do I. You do eat less as you get older, everyone says so.

Besides, he is still so tense, however much he may deny it. He says he is happy, that he has no worries, until we cross swords over something. Then, when the argument looks like getting too intense, he complains that his arm hurts, his stomach hurts, I am making him ill. I think he is using it to get his own way. But I hate conflict, can't bear hurting people, and I am afraid of creating further barriers between us. Invariably I back out, or backtrack.

Nothing is solved. The situation simmers on.

The doctor sends him to a rheumatism specialist to check out his arm. He decides treatment would be unsuitable because it doesn't conform to standard symptoms. If it is no better in a couple of months, he will see him again. Our own doctor prescribes more tablets and white medicine for the digestive problems. I cut down the number of fried meals and he avoids things like apples, or cucumber, or tomatoes.

On one of the rare occasions when he can rally sufficient enthusiasm to visit friends for a meal, he helps himself to one of the taboo foods.

'What about your ulcers?' I hiss.

The husband pricks up his ears.

'Have you got ulcers?' he enquires.

'The doctor says it's either ulcers or cancer of the stomach, and if it's cancer of the stomach there's nothing anybody can do about it,' Pete replies.

I feel as if someone has slapped me, hard, across the face. I don't know who breaks the uncomfortable silence, or how. I don't know how I eat the rest of the meal. I can't remember how Peter talks his way out of the situation.

My mind is whirling with new possibilities, new fears. I stir my coffee in a fury. If the doctor really said that, why didn't he send Peter for tests, however little the medical profession may be able to do? And why didn't Peter share the burden before — and in a less devastating manner?

☆   ☆

The autumn days grow shorter. Half term. Bonfire night. My birthday: the unmentionable one. Peter and I are banished to the lounge while the children cook a celebration meal. All the years of wincing as a chair scrapes across the kitchen floor and a little voice pipes, 'I will help you, mummy,' have a pay-off. Debra (our adopted daughter) is making prawn cocktail, David setting the table, and Margaret cooking pork chops in mustard sauce. Jenny (aged three) is supposed to be helping to make chocolate mousse, until she tells Debra that the egg whites are dirty water, and Debra tips them down the drain. When Margaret discovers what she has done, Jenny is evicted, screaming, from the kitchen.

Apart from that, it is a good evening, one when I can forget the anxiety that still nags at the back of my mind. The new fear, not articulated before that dreadful evening even though it had hovered as a question-mark, to be pushed away as rapidly as possible.

Weight loss, digestive problems, tiredness, loss of muscle power. I shudder. I will not think about it. I always assume the worst. This time the devil is not going to get the better of my imagination. It can only be ulcers. It must be. His father had identical symptoms ten years ago. When he went into hospital for an exploratory operation they diagnosed ulcers, put him on a diet and special medication, and within weeks he was back to normal. Now, at the age of eighty, he chops all their firewood, digs the garden, and shins up the neighbour's sycamore to cut down beansticks, given half a chance.

Besides, we have been warning Peter for years about the way he abuses his body. If you consistently rush meals, never allow proper time for rest and relaxation, and take on responsibility for so many causes that everyone around suffers from jet lag trying to keep up, sooner or later something is going to give. In this case it is the lining of his main digestive organ. It is a common phenomenon amongst over-pressed executives. The doctor is right not to panic. His comment about the other possibility was only his way of telling Peter not to get neurotic about his symptoms.

Anyway, everyone knows that teaching is a stress profession. Ulcers are stress-related. Peter is under stress, whatever he says to the contrary. His body language gives him away. He denies it is work. He is cutting back on other commitments. There are only two more possibilities. Both are too awful to contemplate.

When I worry and fret at the question, he jerks away like a kite on a windy day. I hate myself in the role of the one holding the strings. I lack the necessary skills. I haven't the confidence to enforce my own viewpoint, and my feelings and reactions entangle us in some glorious messes. The easy option would be to cut the cords. Let him go. If it really is me making him ill I must face that option, in the full knowledge of all that it would do to the kids and me. I would not find failure an easy bedfellow. Neither would I be able to live with myself if the other alternative was my fault.

☆     ☆

I dream that the whole family are away at a holiday camp. All is well until we go into some form of crazy house on the fairground. It is like moving through a maze of rooms which are distorted by peculiar angles, and painted harsh shades of red and black, the kind of colours I do not find restful. The walls seem to press in on me. The rooms become progressively smaller. I know there is no going back, but the only way out is through a slit no larger than a letter-box. The children seem unconcerned. They are laughing and shrieking somewhere in the background. I am alone, and becoming increasingly panic stricken. Peter is ahead of me. Somehow he has got out. He is laughing and joking with a friend outside. I know that if he could get through that tiny opening so can I.

'Come on,' he encourages. 'There's nothing to be afraid of.'

My logical mind tells me it is all an illusion. If I push against the letter-box it will probably open, and I will be free. But I dare not do it. I wake screaming, 'I can't. I can't. I can't.'

If dreams are a reflection of our mental state, that is a very accurate portrayal of mine.

✧          ✧

'Oh, God, I don't think I can handle all this,' I grieve one day when the going is particularly tough. 'It's going to destroy us.'

Back comes the answer. 'It is not going to destroy you. It will strengthen you.'

Something needs to. I am running out of resources. Rapidly.

✧          ✧

For my sanity's sake I turn to Len and his wife Shirley to get things into some form of perspective. If I go under, I take four children with me. I must not shut my anxieties inside myself, and tie myself in psychosomatic knots. That will only end in a course of tranquillizers. I know. I have been there before. Unlike Peter, I have learnt from experience that there are limits to what I can take.

'Anxiety neurosis,' is what the doctor will pronounce if I go scuttling to him with a lump in the gullet, or ache in the jaw. It's all so stupid. It makes me so cross with myself. Why do I always expect the worst, feel so threatened by rejection?

A mental picture of my childhood flashes into my mind. An only child. Rarely allowed to play with other children. Sharing a home with grandparents who could not stand the noise and bustle. A loner, desperately wanting friends, never quite knowing how to relate to others my own age. A dreamer, curled in an armchair with a book or puzzle, picking up the vibes of antagonism that flow from my grandmother to my father. Never daring to express an opinion in case it could be used as a weapon to hurt those I love the most.

A great wave of sadness sweeps over me for all the inadequacies that has left behind.

'Weep for that little girl,' says a voice in my head.

Permission to cry? For myself? I don't need to be told twice. The floodgates open. It is a damp, but healing, experience. It makes me more aware of what has made the me that I, and now Peter, find so hard to live with. The problem is . . . can I use this new understanding to help me see why I react as I do, and to grow beyond it?

'Lord, it's all such a mess. We're such complex creatures. We understand so little of one another, of ourselves even. How can I see through to what is going on in Peter when it takes so long to acknowledge what is going on in myself? If only we knew how much of his illness is physical, and how much psychological. We're such weird and wonderful beings, Lord. The mind and body are so closely related. Is it all in my mind? Anxiety? Neurosis?'

Looking at Peter, I think I have every cause to be anxious. Even his hair has gone from silver to white in the last six months. Why can't the doctor see that something is wrong? If I know Peter, he is probably doing his, 'Sorry to bother you. I've got this slight problem,' routine. Maybe I should go with him? But I know what response that suggestion will get.

I try voicing my concern about Peter when I take one of the children for treatment. The doctor doesn't seem particularly perturbed. I don't know whether to be reassured, or even more exasperated. If only Peter would talk about his fears instead of sending me so many double messages.

'What do you think of the new slim-line image?' he jokes, patting his waist with apparent satisfaction.

People cluck approvingly. The expected response.

At home he is on and off the bathroom scales with increasing regularity. He is still losing weight, but it seems sporadic, and directly related to periods of more obvious stress. That figures. I lost nearly a stone when my father was ill. Some people do eat less in times of stress. If I comment about it, he shrugs it away with a 'Don't fuss. I'm OK,' or 'I'm fasting for a friend whose marriage is under stress.'

With a great effort of self-control, I refrain from stating the obvious.

☆      ☆

Christmas looms on the horizon. End of term parties. Concerts. Carols. Endless mince pies. False gaiety. Christmas dinner for the staff at school. Peter bobs up and down, pouring wine, chatting up the cook, the cleaning ladies, the school nurse. Half his dinner remains uneaten and he says he will eat his pudding 'later'. For weeks he has been picking at his evening meal and using the excuse that he's not hungry because he's had a 'big dinner' at school. If it's as much as this, no wonder he's losing weight. I sense that those who are closest to him at school are as uneasy and uncertain as I am. But what to do?

I try to forget my anxieties, divert my energies, stop feeling sorry for myself. I look around for folk who may be missing out on the usual festivities, or giving out to others with little opportunity to relax themselves. We arrange a party. Halfway through, Peter comes home from his school Christmas party. He abandons his motor cycling gear in the garage, and walks into our party dressed as a punk rocker — in a dustbin-liner, hairy legs, silver-sprayed shoes and a wig. The impact is immediate. It's not as if you could miss him at the best of times.

☆      ☆

Peter buys a Christmas tree for church. All fourteen foot of it. He ropes it on the roofrack with me 'helping' in my usual ineffective way. The Almighty never did bless me with a great deal of muscle power. Stamina maybe. Muscles no way. Either I don't pull the ropes tight enough, or I fasten them in the wrong place. It does not make for the kind of feelings Christmas is supposed to engender. I begin to wish this particular custom had never been thought of. When the tree is eventually secure, it stretches the entire length of the car, and I have visions of being pulled in by the police — especially when it slips at one stage, and the driver behind has to do a sudden detour to avoid being pinned on the top as an unwilling angel.

I don't know how Peter manages to get it into an upright position at church, with one arm almost out of action, but manage he does. Get help? Not likely. He balances over the pulpit, hurling strings of tinsel and fairy lights across the branches. What's a drop of ten foot or more? He is used to working forty feet up in the rafters with his pal Ray, doing the re-wiring. And has a pair of broken glasses and an electric shock to prove it.

By the time he has collected his parents from Dorset, wound up the end of term, taken half the burden of the Christmas services, and sent out the final Christmas mailing for the Nefyn mission, he is in a state of near-collapse.

He spends most of Christmas curled in an armchair in the corner of the lounge, sleeping. I do what I can to divert the children, but I am not the life and soul of the party at the best of times. Jenny wades through presents, pantos, a year's supply of chocolate in one session, with all the exuberance of a normal three-year-old. The older ones find the going harder.

'What's the matter with dad?' their eyes signal when he grumphs, puts an abrupt end to their conversations, or slumps across the table in the middle of a meal.

'I wish I knew,' my shoulders reply.

His parents are equally anxious. I hear myself reassuring them.

'It's a virus. Christmas is always a hectic time for teachers. He does too much.'

'He's at a funny age,' says his mother.

You can say that again.

☆        ☆

I look towards the New Year with a sense of dread.

'Where will it all end, Lord?'

On second thoughts, don't answer that.

I'd rather not know.

We go shopping in the January sales. Peter tries on jackets and trousers.

'What do you think?' he asks. 'Shall I buy them? Is it OK?'

I feel he is asking, 'Am I OK? Will I have a chance to wear them?'

I smile and tell him he looks good.

He does. Seeing him standing in the shop, broad-shouldered, lop-sided grin, I would fall for him just as easily as I did twenty years ago. Even with the knowledge of how infuriating we find each other at times.

If I can do anything to allay the fears that must be lurking at the back of his mind, I will — even if it drains my emotional energy to the dregs. When needs must, I am as capable as the next at assuming a mask. Probably more so. I got plenty of training with my grandmother in my early days.

It is perhaps just as well.

☆     ☆

Each day has become an incredible balancing act. Trying to harmonize the needs of two eighty-year-olds, three teenagers, a three-year-old and a sick husband is tough going. And that's making no allowance for the 'I' that pops its own discordant note into the general clamour with frightening regularity.

It is nearly twelve months since dad died. I must keep on the move. Not sink into self-pity. Peter, I need you. I loved my dad. He isn't there any more. I didn't know what a great gap it would leave, how much I would miss him. Help me. Please.

☆     ☆

It is a family joke that granny and grandad Green come for Christmas and stay till Easter. That is a slight exaggeration. It's half term when they go home, usually. We try to keep them till the worst of the bad weather is over. At least, that's the theory. In practice it usually snows the day after they go back to Dorset.

Grandad Green follows me up the garden one day, as I go to hang out the washing.

'I don't know if I ought to tell you this,' he says. 'But when Jenny was chatting this morning, she said, "When people die, they don't come back, do they?"'

My heart freezes. Poor little kid. I am not alone in my grief. We forget how bright she is, how quickly she picks up clues from fragments of conversation. She must have heard us talking about grandad Williams, and slotted the memories together.

No Jenny. They do not come back, unfortunately for us. It hurts, doesn't it.

A memory of the morning after my father's death flits across my mind. Jenny staring at the orange tooth mug mother is about to throw in the bin.

'I loved Dennis the Menace,' she said.

We put her comment on her posy of flowers for the funeral. What better tribute could any grandfather want, or those who had also loved him wish to hear . . . no matter how many the tears?

Now I have to comfort the other grandad, allay his fears, assure him I will chat to Jenny. Our mixed blessing. The one my mother was convinced was sent for a purpose.

'You'll enjoy this one, be more relaxed,' friends comforted, when I rebelled at the late pregnancy and all the restrictions a new baby would impose. 'Besides, the children will help.'

'Ring the other one. It's got bells on,' was my sceptical retort.

But they had been right. I was more relaxed. The children did help. And Peter was over the moon. Even when the baby, with the usual contrariness of the newborn, arrived twenty-four hours after he had left to run the Nefyn mission. In fact, so great was his excitement when the vicar's wife cycled down to relay the news, he rushed into the village, realized he hadn't combed his hair, went to remedy the situation and broke his glasses.

In consequence he arrived back at my mother's home in an old pair held on with a piece of elastic tied round the back of his head. The dressing-down he received from my mother when he said he was coming to see us in hospital like that has gone down in the annals of family history.

Fortunately it did little to quell his exuberance. Soon the whole ward was enjoying the account, before we settled down to the more serious stuff of marvelling at the cause of all the trouble, sleeping in her short shimmy in the 'goldfish tank' beside the bed.

'Well done . . . for thirty-six,' announced a banner marched into the ward by my cousin Ann, the nearest I have ever got to a sister.

It should have read, 'Well done, Ann.'

Her husband and little girl had been killed in a car accident only six months before. To see me with a new baby must have been sheer torture. It had always been me, the pessimist, who had dreaded losing one of my family, despite the fact that I was the one born with the silver spoon in my mouth while nothing ever seemed to go right for her.

'You do realize you're the only woman left in our family with a man, don't you?' she informed me, one day after my father died. It had not escaped my notice.

I shiver. But it is not with chill of the wind. I peg out the washing, furiously. I will not think. I will not consider the possibility. Peter is going to be OK. There is nothing wrong with our marriage. This is just a temporary setback. We are planning a holiday. THE holiday. We are going to France in the summer on our holiday of a lifetime. Our first ever summer one. We have pored over maps and details of ferry time-tables. We are booked into a cottage halfway down the western coast of France. I am not happy about the distance, but Peter reckons we can break the journey and I can share the driving. The thought of driving on the other side of the road and going the wrong way round a French roundabout is giving me nightmares already, but everyone else seems to think it is highly amusing. Whether they will be quite so amused when we get hauled in by the French police remains to be seen.

'If you ever get that far,' nags the little gremlin at the back of my mind.

I refuse to listen. Concentrate on brushing up your French, Wendy, and fantasizing about cheap wine, French cooking, and no responsibilities.

End of January. Peter's birthday. He passed the forty milestone last year. We celebrated in style, with a party culminating at midnight with a cake covered in forty candles, and lime sorbet drenched with Asti Spumante. 'Fizzy pudding' Jenny and Peter named it, as he fed her spooonfuls when she was woken by the noise and general excitement.

This year it is a quieter affair. The budget will only stretch to such mammoth events once a decade. Even if Peter were fit enough.

We will have a family celebration on Sunday, so Peter and I claim Saturday evening for ourselves. We try a local Greek restaurant several have recommended. Over the food and wine Peter relaxes. He samples asparagus, and seems to have no problems with eating, for once. I am relieved. At least he is not likely to nod off to sleep in the middle of the meal here. I wonder, for a moment, if they have that problem at school. I very much doubt it.

Getting him to sit still for more than three minutes is the more usual story. For all his administrative ability, he does not yet seem to have learned the meaning of the word delegation. He must be headmaster, electrician, supply staff, first-aid expert, carpenter, games master, marriage counsellor and general dogsbody, all rolled into one. And that's before he starts on all the committees and conferences that he organizes for the education authority.

Oh, well. He must be what he is. Even if it is exasperating. I switch my attention back to the present. He is talking. About school, yes, but also about himself, his health. I prick up my ears. It is the first time I have heard him acknowledge anything remotely resembling concern. It is too good an opportunity to miss.

'If you are not satisfied, you must go back to the doctor,' I insist. 'Spell it out to him. Make him listen. He knows you are an intelligent man. Surely he would expect you to go back if you thought there was anything seriously wrong?'

He listens, but I don't know if he has received the message.

On Monday he is home from school by five o'clock. Unheard of occurrence.

'I'm going to the doctor,' he announces.

I give him a kiss and a hug of approval.

It's a blessing it is nearly time for the evening meal. With eight to feed there is little time to sit and brood. Mercifully. He returns just as we are about to eat. I corner him in the corridor for a couple of seconds, out of earshot of the rest of the family.

'How did it go?' I enquire.

'He says he doesn't think there's anything to worry about,' he replies casually. 'But he's sending me to the Hospital, to set all our minds at rest.'

I suppress an 'About time too,' and give him another hug.

At last something is happening. It is an enormous relief.

Our Bible reading that evening is Psalm 29. The imagery is that of a thunderstorm, climaxing in the lines 'The Lord gives strength to his people. The Lord blesses his people with peace.'

The Bible-reading notes we use speak of God being in control, even in times of greatest danger and stress. The moments of greatest upheaval are often the occasion for a new vision of God's majesty.

Is it a warning of storms still to come, or the quiet calm when the worst is over? Either way, it is reassuring. 'You are in control, Lord. We have always been very conscious of that fact, even when it hasn't seemed like it. Now Pete is going to see a specialist. Help us to cling to your strength. And your peace . . .'

☆          ☆

The storm is far from over. Eight hours' rest and we are back in the thick of it. I hear a thud and an 'ouch' as Peter goes down the stairs.

'Are you OK?' I shout from the bathroom.

'I missed a step,' comes the reply.

That night he comes back from the school in agony. He bent to pick up a bunch of keys and felt his back click. He crawls into bed. We know from a previous bout of disc trouble that the doctors will only prescribe bed rest. Great. Now he has ulcers, a gammy arm, and a bad back to contend with.

On Sunday, grandad, not to be outdone, has a bad turn in church. Chris, my nurse friend, administers a cup of tea reassurance, and some good advice. I doubt that he will listen. We all know where Peter's energy and obstinacy come from!

☆ ☆

The next month Peter goes to see the specialist. He seems reassured. He won't let me go with him, but reports that the specialist reckons it is probably 'acid'. He has a barium meal check. He copes all right on the actual day, but his back is still bad, he has various aches and pains, and his eating habits deteriorate even further. Our own doctor prescribes some different medicine for the digestive problems, and I buy Complan, glucose, anything I can think of to get some nourishment into him. A friend, battling with similar problems with her husband, has worked her way through seven packets of Complan since Christmas, by sneaking it into soups and drinks. I can't get even one into Peter.

The children at his school were once asked to draw a pet they thought most suitable for each of the teachers. A perceptive child chose a bloodhound for Peter, because you could never get away with anything with Mr Green. I know the feeling.

☆ ☆

We go to Worcestershire, to my mother, for half term. Peter is not really up to it, but it would have been my father's birthday, and mother needs us. Besides, Ann, at last, has cause for celebration. She is to marry someone who is bringing stability and hope into her life, after all the sadness and several abortive attempts to forget. They hold a grand engagement party: a slap-up meal for sixty in the upstairs room of a pub tucked under the armpit of Pershore Abbey. There is laughter, chatter, friends and family. The last three occasions we have all been together have not been a cause for rejoicing. Now we can let our hair down. Jenny, and the little girl who is becoming part of Ann's family, dance under a revolving sphere which scatters diamonds of multi-coloured light around the room.

Ann's mother tries to partner the older girls off with Ann's sons' friends. She grabs David and hauls him round the dance floor. Next time she comes near he retreats under the table. If she downs any more of the brandies Ann's farmer friends are plying her with, I am afraid she will be joining him.

I drink several for her, joking that it is to stop her getting drunk. In reality it is to blot out the sight of Peter, who would normally be at the heart of the festivities, finding it as much as he can do to sit on the chair and keep his eyes open. He is wearing the jacket and trousers he bought in the January sales, and has a fixed smile on his face. To anyone who knows him on a superficial level he is still Peter, the capable broad-shouldered, six-footer, willing to carry the woes of the world, or at least share the weight of the journey for a few yards. Those of us who know him slightly better are beginning to wonder if we are going to have to carry him home, but it will not be because of the alcohol. He has hardly drunk more than half a glass of lemonade all evening.

'What's the matter with Pete?' my uncle asks.

If only we knew.

☆      ☆

Peter has pinned so much hope in the hospital people, but even they seem to be dragging their heels. They said he would receive an appointment to discuss the results of the tests with the specialists within two weeks.

Each day seems an eternity. Peter can hardly wait to get back to London to see if there is anything in the post.

The car is less enthusiastic. Like me, it is a slow starter in the morning. Peter sits, tensed, in the passenger seat, becoming increasingly frustrated by my ineptness and his lack of mobility. My mother and aunt peer anxiously through the car windows. The children sit in the back, frozen into silence. Even Jenny. The situation is bad. The more Peter tells me what I should, or should not, be doing, the more uptight I become. I know I am not mechanically minded but, rightly or wrongly, when I do things my way at least I can get the wretched thing started. This way we look like being here till kingdom come — if I haven't done something drastic before then.

I am just on the point of taking myself a walk round the block while we both simmer down, when the engine hiccups into life. Doing it my way.

☆　　☆

My mother telephones in the evening to check that we have arrived home safely.

'We were beginning to wonder if you were going to make it,' she says.

So was I.

☆　　☆

There is no news from the hospital. Peter looks awful. His cheeks are almost drained of colour. He is in constant pain with his back. The painkillers the doctor gives him make little impression.

'Lord, can't somebody *do* something?'

☆　　☆

Peter goes to an osteopath. When he had disc trouble before, an osteopath was the one who finally got him on his feet, in two sessions. I don't say anything but, judging by his emaciated form and lack of muscle power, it is going to take more than manipulation to set him to rights this time. It is as if his body is expressing what his words deny. He cannot settle comfortably to sleep.

The only thing that seems to bring him any relief is a hot bath. Then at last he begins to unwind a little.

'What if the specialist says it is tension?' I summon courage to ask, one day.

Pete dismisses any such possibility, and jokes about being 'laid back.'

That's news to me. Most of the time he is so uptight I am constantly manoeuvring the older children out of 'answering back' range — especially the one whose only line of defence is to shout louder than the other two.

The car is due, if not overdue, for its Ministry of Transport roadworthiness test, but he won't tell me where the certificate is, or what to do. If we come anywhere near discussing the source of our underlying tension, he diverts the conversation or clams up completely.

'Why do you worry me about minor problems?' he asks. 'I need to relax, not worry.'

I cannot let him get away with that one.

'Do you relax by pretending problems don't exist, or by facing up to them?' I reply.

He doesn't answer.

☆       ☆

The trouble is, how far can you push? Peter is so obviously ill. Every fibre in me wants to work for his healing. But can healing be bought by avoiding the uncomfortable, the unpleasant?

'I don't know whether to submerge him in tender loving care, or give him a kick in the pants,' I agonize to a friend.

She talks about firm, loving care. It makes sense. So do the scriptures.

Afterwards, when he has been to hospital, and they have decided the appropriate treatment for these blessed ulcers we will get to the root of all these tensions. There is no way we are going on like this. What point are operations, medication, if they don't deal with the underlying stress?

☆       ☆

Peter has his appointment to see the specialist. If we can just hold on one more week. Protect without being fussy.

We work out a rota to transport him backwards and forwards to school. Driving the Honda is out of the question. Even he can see that. He hasn't wanted to handle the car for some weeks. He says there is something wrong with the tracking but it doesn't seem any harder to manoeuvre to me. I guess it's lack of muscle power and that gammy left arm, though he would hate to admit it. Defeat is not a word which exists in Peter's vocabulary.

☆       ☆

Peter preaches at church on Sunday. I am thankful I am

out teaching Sunday school. I don't know how he can stand, let alone preach.

☆ ☆

At school Peter sits in a corner of his office where he is less likely to be noticed and inundated with every hassle from a blocked toilet through to a family crisis which is affecting one or several of the children in his care.

As at home, sometimes it works, sometimes it doesn't. Even when chained to their post, bloodhounds let very little escape their notice, and this particular breed still finds it very hard to stay confined to his kennel for more than ten minutes. Or to relinquish authority.

Mention of anything which he would normally be organizing, or ignoring, soon raises every hackle to a defensive position. Stocktaking, income tax, school journey, the church accounts, that wretched MOT for the car are all taboo subjects. It does not make for restful nights.

Neither does the thought of the impending hospital appointment. What will the tests have revealed? How will the doctors start treating the symptoms, restoring his lost vitality? Peter seems to be thinking in terms of a couple of weeks. I guess it is more likely to be months before he is fully in action again. What hell must he be going through, if the fear of cancer is still hovering at the back of his mind? No wonder he can't sleep.

One night, as we lie in the darkness, he expresses a feeling of 'nothingness'. The painkillers are hardly touching the ache in his back. His movement is severely limited. He has always been able to sleep almost as his head touches the pillow. The night horrors are a new, and unwelcome, experience.

☆ ☆

The night before Peter is due to see the specialist, his back goes into a spasm. He cannot move forwards or backwards. I am useless at moving or lifting anything heavier than a couple of bags of grocery, and Peter is over eleven stone. Still. He does not like it, but I have to wake our son to help move him into a relatively comfortable position.

☆     ☆

The next morning he still cannot move, and is due at the hospital by 11.30. If we cancel the appointment it means more delays, more distress. Peter insists I phone the osteopath, to see if he can do anything. As expected the osteopath is reluctant, to say the least. He suggests we contact our doctor to see if the hospital will give him the results of the tests. It is possible, but not very probable.

Peter's deputy arrives with some papers from school for him to sign.

Chris, the nurse, takes her children to playgroup and comes to administer what help she can. With a combination of massage, prayer, gentle persuasion and specialized lifting skills, we eventually get Peter on his feet and dressed.

☆     ☆

Waiting at the hospital is unbearable. Peter can hardly walk, but he cannot sit still. The hours drag by. Eventually, when the clinic is nearly empty, and the doctors leaving for lunch, his name is called. I take his arm. This time I am going with him. There will be no arguments.

The specialist pronounces.

'Inflammation of the stomach.'

A card is in the post. They want him in for further tests. A bed will be available on Sunday.

'But . . . it's taken three of us to get him here this morning,' I protest. 'He's in agony with his back and shoulder. Can't anything be done now?'

The specialist hesitates, asks Peter some more questions, examines his shoulder.

'I'll see if we can get a bed,' he says, 'if you can get a porter to wheel him over to the admissions desk.'

☆     ☆

After several false starts, they manage to locate a bed. A young doctor examines Peter.

'Relax,' she says. 'I can't examine you. You're so tense. What are you afraid of?'

☆ ☆

I wake early. Too early. Peter's half of the bed is empty. Peter is in hospital. I am alone. There is no need to act, pretend, bottle up my feelings. The tensions of the last few months overflow into several handkerchiefs. By the time the worst is over, dawn is beginning to lighten the curtains. An image from a decade and a half ago clicks into my mind. Easter Sunday morning in hospital, with Margaret just a week old. Me fretting to be home with the rest of the family. The nurse bustling into the room with a cup of tea, tugging back the curtains. Black fir trees silhouetted against a flamingo dawn. The consciousness of the Lord's presence so close I almost expected to see his footprints in the dew.

'Lord, I need that kind of experience now, some assurance of your presence.'

I climb out of bed, expectantly, and pull back the curtains.

The sky is grey. At the bottom of our garden a sycamore tree stands stark and emaciated, like Peter, like the *pietà*. It is as if God is saying, 'Close the curtains. Get back into bed. It isn't time for the resurrection yet.'

For once I do as I am told. There is a great ache in my heart. I think of the darkness before Easter Sunday. I soak a few more handkerchiefs, and the pillow, and the continental quilt.

It stands me in good stead for the day.

By the time I have howled that lot out of my system I can cope with Jenny's questions, the anxieties of the grand-parents, the need everyone has to retain some form of normality. I cook meals, wash clothes, ferry people backwards and forwards to the hospital, joke with the other visitors, even feign interest in the football scores.

Part of me is lying in a hospital bed, waiting, wondering . . . But at least he is not in such severe pain now. Already the various drugs are beginning to take effect. He is smiling again, and teasing the nurses. I might have known that would perk him up, if nothing else would.

☆　　☆

Only school and Sunday school are beyond me. The children teach me far more than I am capable of teaching them. No wonder the kingdom of God belongs to those with such uncomplicated faith and love.

I take a class at Peter's school one afternoon a week. When the children have come to the end of their questions about Mr Green they move spontaneously into praying for him. One after the other. It is a humbling experience, and only one measure of the depth of love he has helped build in one small corner of London.

☆　　☆

One of the priests responsible for the school visits Peter most evenings. He summons me for a chat. When I know the depth of his concern for Peter, my own anxieties bubble out, uninhibited. I share my early morning experience — the hope of the resurrection.

He is silent for a moment.

'There's more than one kind of resurrection, you know,' he says gently.

Ah. Indeed there is. And I hadn't even considered the possibility.

'No, Lord. Not that. You wouldn't. Would you? Not Pete? Please!'

☆　　☆

Somehow I take my leave and drive through the Sunday evening streets. I can't go home in this state. The family must fend for themselves. They know where to look for food, and surely someone will have the sense to put Jenny to bed.

I head for openness, space . . . the stretch of grassland dividing our downtown area from the more select suburbs. The sun is setting. There are trees and water, even if it is only a glorified duckpond. In the strange half-light of early evening, I sob out my anguish.

There are people I could go to, but this is so big I can take it only to the One who has been my strength, my security, for more than a quarter of a century. Slowly his peace sinks into me. The sobs ease. I am able to go back to the hospital for evening visiting, and face Peter.

A fellow headmaster is with him. They chat about schools, family, the Inner London Education Authority. When he has gone it is good just to sit together and hold hands. Peter is tired and whoozy with the drugs but he is calmer, less distant. We pray together, committing him into the keeping of those hands that possess so much more skill and power than all the resources of the medical profession.

When the bell goes for the end of visiting, Peter insists on walking to the lift. Seeing him swaying down the corridor, it is all I can do to fight back the tears.

Could the priest be right? What if the doctors cannot restore him to health and strength?

The big question I have kept pushing to the back of my mind for months leaps into prominence. Peter's limp arm and wasted body are more obvious now that he has only pyjamas, rather than padded jackets, to camouflage the effect his illness has had on his body. I want to hold him in my arms, force some strength into him, tell him how much we need and love him.

'Oh, God, how can I? Hasn't he enough to contend with, without having my dependent needs piled on top?'

Halfway down the corridor, Peter pauses. Our arms go round one another.

'I miss you,' I hear my voice murmuring. 'A hot-water bottle and the pillow are not nearly such good company.'

He hugs me closer.

'I'll be home soon,' he says.

☆     ☆

The days move on in a mist of visits, visitors, X-rays, tests, fruit, flowers, letters, cards. Peter has an exploratory operation, a gastroscopy. None of us can remember how to pronounce it, but we know all the details. Grandad went through the same procedure a decade ago. The story is

41

part of family folklore, including the joyful conclusion when the doctors came to give him the results.

'It's good news, Mr Green,' he repeats. 'You haven't got cancer.'

He always seems surprised that they had even suspected it.

'I was lucky,' he confides. 'I didn't have to have an operation. That's when the trouble starts. When they cut you open.'

The words strike home with new meaning, horrifying possibilities.

'Lord. Peter. What will the biopsy reveal? What will they do to him?'

The wise words of a friend who had to face a similar mountain just before Christmas soothe my fears a little.

'If it's the worst, there's nothing you can do about it,' she advised. 'And if it's not, why worry?'

Precisely.

I defy the devil and all his attacks on my imagination by walking under two sets of ladders on the way to the bank. I do not believe in bad luck. One was on my behalf. The other on Peter's.

At four o'clock in the morning, I am less brave. It is becoming a regular ritual to howl my eyes out to the accompaniment of the dawn chorus. Ah well. It sets me up for the day. I am less likely to collapse in tears at whatever the next twenty hours manage to hurl at me.

At least the main pressure is off, now Peter is so much more relaxed. When he's happy we all cope a lot better. It is a delight to see him chatting up the nurses and shocking the more sheltered of our friends with some of the cards he has received.

Two hundred, three hundred, five hundred. The post floods in by the bagful. There is room for only a fraction, the specials, on the locker by his bed. Someone suggests stringing the surplus round the bed and across the wall, but Peter is embarrassed by all the attention he is receiving compared to the other patients in the ward. He cannot understand why everyone is being so kind — until the content of the messages begins to sink in. Page after page tells of what he has done for people, the influence he has had on their lives, how he has helped them to know God.

It is a very rare privilege to know how much we mean to people. Most of us go through life thinking other folk just about tolerate us. He now knows beyond a doubt just how greatly he is loved and respected.

The thought reduces him to tears. Frequently.

☆       ☆

It is a generally damp month all round. The words of the hymn, 'O joy that seekest me through pain,' are taking on a new dimension. The rainbows that trace their way through the rain of our tears are a peculiar blend of hope, despair, pain, joy, disbelief.

☆       ☆

Beneath it all, we cling to the hope of Easter. I take Jenny and Debra for a walk in the woods. We pick Peter a bunch of alder catkins.

'A sure and certain sign,' I promise as I kiss him.

The children buy him the largest, shiniest Easter egg they can afford. He keeps it in a prominent position on his table, along with their photographs.

Jenny scribbles him a note, or a picture, every day. The general gist seems to be, 'I love you, daddy. Hope you're getting better.'

The older ones are more reserved in their approach. Hospital visiting cannot come easily to teenagers still struggling to come to terms with the social graces, and none of ours are particularly communicative on the superficial level, which is all the hospital set-up manages to allow. They make a valiant effort but conversation always flows more freely at the weekend, when the antics of West Ham and the other football clubs are the main topic of conversation.

Fortunately they, too, are more relaxed now Peter is in less pain and they all have plenty to keep them occupied. David is taking his 'O' level exams in a couple of months. Margaret is at the stage when girl friends are important. Chat about boys, clothes, the pop scene, parties, and the occasional half hour of homework occupy most evenings for her, and her mate, who is rapidly becoming an extra member of our family. I am pleased. Margaret needs someone around for her. It cannot be easy being squashed between two powerful personalities. So far her main form of retaliation has been to shout louder than they do. This has always gone down a bomb with the member of the family who has the loudest voice of the lot. It is always 'Margaret' who manages to get the full force of his wrath, regardless who starts the trouble — and Margaret, surprisingly, who is not afraid to answer him back. It is not by accident that she bought him a Snoopy mug for his fortieth birthday, with the words 'Nobody understands my generation either' printed on the side.

Deb is a different entity. She is our other 'special', and has been a member of our family since she was five months old. You always know exactly what she is thinking. If she is happy, her whole face is alight. If she is angry, you get out of the way. Rapidly. Or send for reinforcements. No one is going to walk over her without a fight, and rightly so. From infancy she has had to contend with remarks such as 'My brother says you're a nig-nog,' when she was playing quietly on the sand, harming no one.

As she moves into her teens, life is not going to be plain sailing for her. She does not suffer injustices gladly, and I fear for her in a society which too often assesses people by the colour of their skin rather than by the quality of their personality.

So far Peter has always been around to take her under his wing when the going has been tough. How does she feel now, with those all-sheltering wings so severely pinioned? There is little time to talk, with all the rush of visiting and people. But on the morning of the exploratory operation it was Deb who prayed. 'Lord, don't let him be frightened.'

At the moment I am still doing my best to keep the children's fears at bay. But for all our sakes we have got to get our priorities and relationships right when Peter comes out of hospital. Too much is at stake to mess around in these crucial teenage years.

I have another dream in the early hours of one morning. We are driving along an approach road to a motorway. As we reach the roundabout leading on to it we can see that the motorway ahead is blocked with several lanes of traffic, all at a standstill. To join the stream would be foolishness, but how do we make Peter understand?

We are debating what we should do when a child's voice suddenly pipes from the back seat, 'But we're not going in the right direction anyway.'

I await the response with baited breath. Will Peter ignore the suggestion, or ram the car into the dandelions in the middle of the roundabout?

To everyone's amazement he says simply, as if waking out of a reverie, 'No. Of course we're not,' and turns the car in a different direction.

If only it were that simple. But it is a straw to cling on to, a possibility of better things to come.

☆    ☆

Fortunately granny and grandad seem more relaxed now that Peter is receiving proper attention. The last three months must have been hard going for them. It looks as if this year they really will be with us till Easter. Having seen their only child pulled so low, it is understandable they need to stay to see him on the way to recovery.

The letters and cards are already a great comfort to them. They spend hours poring through the piles I take home each day. We even manage to winkle granny out of the house for the occasional visit to the hospital, which is no mean achievement. She is always very self-conscious when there are strangers around. At home she will bolt for the bedroom when the doorbell rings, or we have friends round for a meal.

To visit Peter you have to fight your way through teachers, headteachers, inspectors, divisional officers, clergy, nuns, and a miscellany of admirers he has managed to accumulate in his ten years' involvement in the inner city. He is running a daily book, clocking up the number of visits from the education, religious, and 'other' professions.

We do not begrudge him the visitors (Peter has always needed people, and thrives on all the attention and mental diversion), provided that he and the others have sense to realize his family need him too . . . if only for a few precious minutes at the end of visiting.

Fortunately the weekends are slightly quieter, and granny can sneak near enough to hold his hand, or just sit near him.

Grandad does not have these problems. Like Peter, he loves company . . . especially the female variety. He is in his element with all the young nurses and teachers. I sometimes wonder how granny feels about it, and if I will still be suffering the same mixture of amusement and frustration if Peter still follows in his footsteps at eighty. To look at him you would never dream he had had three major setbacks in the last ten years.

At first sight, granny looks by far the frailer. Five foot of nothing. How she has nursed him through the various illnesses, heaven only knows. They must have bred them tough at the turn of the century. One blessing, I have braved Peter's wrath and changed doctors, and she is the first to benefit. She had been becoming increasingly deaf, and the frustration this caused between her and grandad would not have made for happy living when they return to Dorset. The new doctor looked immediately for wax, had her ears syringed by the nurse, and as we walked back into the house she could hear the radio playing in the kitchen. Now grandad is in trouble for shouting at her, and turning up the radio and television too loud. Ah well. You can't win 'em all.

The new doctor didn't take long to work out the situation. I reckon he deserves a special medal for taking our family under his wing. Four children, two temporary senior residents, a neurotic woman, and a man he has never met who is likely to need several months of intensive treatment before he is restored to normality, must be sufficient to daunt the staunchest spirit.

Happily it looks as if it takes a fair amount to ruffle his feathers. Pete may have difficulty accepting the fact that I have acted on my own initiative, but I think he will find a kindred spirit in this capable man with kind eyes — even if he would rather die than admit it.

Peter has never found it easy to delegate authority. Having to hand over responsibility for school must be agony. It has been so large a part of his life, as the Nefyn mission was. It must feel as if suddenly all the things that are important to him, that have helped to give him identity, are being prised one by one from his reluctant fingers.

I try to deal with as many domestic issues as possible without drawing them to his attention. But somebody, sooner or later, usually manages to give me away. I find the MOT certificate for the car, at last. It expired in January. A friend at church tells me what to do. As I guessed, the scrunched-up front headlight is illegal and must be replaced. It's a wonder we haven't been pulled in by the police long ago. So much for Peter's 'Nothing to worry about.' It's been like it for so long, I can't even remember how it happened.

Oh . . . yes . . . I can. The night dad died. The emergency phone-call, the mad dash across London to catch the last train, someone pulling out of a junction, then braking suddenly, and Peter crunching into the rear of his car. Oh well, it's all water under the bridge by now. The car is being mended. The memories are not so easily dealt with.

Neither is Peter. Surprisingly, when someone lets slip about the car he hardly turns a hair. But he is not going to give in about the cheque book. He has always dealt with the major bills and can see no necessity for explaining such trivialities as rates, mortgage, heating payments and the like to such feather-minded mortals as I am. His philosophy has always been to wait for the reminder before a bill is paid. Mine is to get rid of the wretched thing as quickly as possible, especially as we have twice had the gas board at the door threatening to cut off the gas. I know he balances out which bills should be paid which month in his head, but it is not exactly reassuring when they simply disappear into his locker drawer, especially with the volume of post he is receiving. We sail pretty close to the wind each month, but I have no idea what our actual income and expenditure is, especially now he is receiving sickness benefit rather than the usual monthly salary. If I try to discuss the subject he shuts up like a clam. I suppose it is hardly surprising. It is too painful a reminder that he is out of action, not fully in control. I am not going to push the matter. We shall manage, somehow.

'Are we rich?' Debra had a disconcerting habit of asking when she was smaller. 'Or are we poor?'

I usually countered by trying to explain about comparisons and values. I don't know how much she took in, but I think she got the message that we had 'sufficient' for basics, though there was never any to throw around, and all the extras such as Christmas, holidays, outings, shoes, were usually covered by my income. Thank God we have that to tide us over. I shall simply deal with all the bills I can without even mentioning them. When the fire from heaven descends, at least it will be one almighty conflagration, and not a series of irritating sparks. Peter has enough battles to fight with his bodily limitations and the gradual letting go of his other positions of power.

Not that he has any intention of sitting idly in his armchair, watching the world go past. Already he is moulding other spheres of influence for himself, building up relationships with his fellow patients, becoming involved in their concerns: the lad in the next bed who is only fourteen and fed-up to the back teeth in a ward of adult males; the man whose family are in the West Country and can only afford to visit on a special day such as his birthday. If I sneak in to see Peter out of visiting hours the nurses invariably have to organize a search party because he is off on one of his 'visitations'. Fair enough. It must be an incredibly long day, and he has always needed people, activity. Provided that he still has some strength and interest left for us at the end of it, and is not pushing his body too far. As usual.

The combination of visits, visitors, hospital routine, short nights and powerful medication are taking their toll. Sometimes it is an effort for him even to keep his eyes open, with those for whom he would normally put on the 'I-am-in-control-whatever-appearances-may-suggest-to-the-contrary' routine. Often with us he does not even try. I tell myself that it is a compliment, that he feels secure in our company, knows there is no need to put on an act. But when someone comes, and he spends half an hour talking to them with light and enthusiasm in his eyes, it is hard to bear. It may be selfish, but after coming so low on the list of priorities for so long, I am digging in my heels.

'Don't forget us,' I warn one day, when he has phoned umpteen others but never dreamed that we too might like to know the latest reports on him. 'It's as if half of me is missing, with you away.'

'And possibly going on an even longer journey,' adds a little voice at the back of my head. I shake it away.

He pats my hand apologetically. 'I can't always get the phone,' he says. 'And I feel selfish if I hog it too long. Especially when it is the only way those from a distance can contact their folks.'

Now it is my turn to apologize. There are always two sides to every story. If only he would show me the other side of the page a little more often.

☆    ☆

Peter has been in hospital ten days. It feels like ten months. We are still waiting for the results of the exploratory tests, and the pressures are beginning to tell. A combination of late nights, early mornings, household routine, the struggle to do some work, and the emotional burdens of the entire family leave me feeling rather frayed round the edges . . . to say the least.

I stagger in from hospital one day to find World War Three about to erupt between the older generation, and one of the teenagers. I am too tired to go into all the rights and wrongs with the offending youngster. I just burst into tears on her shoulder, and say, 'Love, I need your help.'

I don't know which of us is most taken aback. Wendy? The proud one? The loner? Admitting to needing help?

But there's no way round it. I do. I sometimes feel as if I am the fragile base of a large, inverted pyramid. If I crumble, the whole lot will collapse. There is no way I can carry the load alone. Already I am leaning on a lot of people. The ones whose prayers and expressions of understanding are carrying us along on a great wave of love. Those who have assessed the practical needs and are sharing some of the burdens. The 'listening ears' who are taking the inner fears that I am trying my hardest not to transfer onto the family. If there is real cause for concern, that will be soon enough to share it with them. 'Dear God, let it not be necessary.'

☆     ☆

I pick up one of the colds that travel around families every couple of months. That is all I need. Now I can communicate with Peter only from the foot of the bed, for fear he picks up the germs. And the ache in my face, which is always worse when I am overtired, or the weather is bad, or I am unwell, will become unbearable. Great. Let's get it all over in one go, be thoroughly miserable all round!

Ray, who is keeping a fatherly eye on us all on Peter's behalf, pops in to see how we are faring. He takes one look at me and orders me to bed with a mug of hot milk laced with some of grandad's Christmas present whisky.

I glow in the warmth of someone caring without being fussy. Just a little thing, but it is what I needed — some energy and love being put back into me.

Next day I am on my feet again. Well, if that's what you can call the grim clinging to God, without whom I would surely have gone under long ago. Twenty-five years of experience have taught me to hold on to the fact that he is in control, and he does know what he is doing, however unlikely it may feel. I certainly have more confidence in him than in the doctors. I am afraid my confidence in the medical profession is rapidly being eroded. If I ask to speak to someone, they are either not available, or are too busy, or say they have told my husband.

Yes, but what? If I ask him, he is equally evasive. I think he is still hearing what he wants to hear. I want to get to the root of the illness, make sure it is dealt with, once and for all. There is no way they are going to treat him for ulcers — if it is ulcers — only to have him back in hospital again in a couple of years.

Halfway through afternoon visiting, a young houseman comes to the bed.

'You wanted to see me, Mrs Green?' he says.

I did. But I didn't particularly want a public display of the fact.

When I get back Peter is furious.

'Why should you disturb his tea-break?' he rages. 'What can you tell him that he doesn't know already?'

I say I am just making sure that we get all the information accurate this time. It's all so stupid. Why can't they see husbands and wives together in the first place? Why not cut out all possibility of crossed communications, treat you as responsible adults, instead of naughty children, to be thrown a snippet of information occasionally, just to stop you making too much fuss? I think of dad. The first heart attack. The false reassurance. 'It's nothing to panic about. He'll be back at work by Christmas.' Mother waiting outside the room when he goes back for a check-up, watching, wondering. Why is he so long? Why are so many doctors going in and out? What did they really tell him? If it's all so straightforward, why isn't he getting any better? Then their own doctor, six months later, after the second attack, signing the death certificate, and saying casually, 'Of course, you know it was a massive heart attack he had last August.'

No. We did *not* know. And if dad had known, would he have pushed his body so far the day that he died, trying to prove that he was fit enough to go back to work?

☆          ☆

The results of the gastroscopy are due today. 'Lord, what are they going to say?'

☆          ☆

I ask to see the doctor on my way into the ward.

'We've spoken to your husband,' he says. 'He will tell you.'

Will he? Thump.

He is surrounded by the usual visitors, a group of teachers chatting about school affairs. I am grateful for the interest and light that they bring into his day, but I sit on the bed in a suspension of agony, willing them to go.

'They're going to operate,' Peter suddenly informs the assembled company. Everyone looks at me.

'On what?' I eventually manage to croak.

'How should I know?' Peter shrugs. 'The ulcers I suppose. Why don't you ask the doctors? You're well in with them.'

☆ ☆

At home everyone looks up expectantly when I walk into the lounge.

'They're going to operate,' I hear myself telling them.

'On what?' grandad asks.

'Ulcers,' I reply tersely and, in a most un-Wendy-like public display of emotion, fling my arms around granny's neck, burst into tears, and sob, 'Thank God, it isn't cancer.'

☆ ☆

'They're going to operate.' 'It's when they cut you open the trouble starts.' 'It's good news, Mr Green. You haven't got cancer. We're not going to have to operate.'

The words whirl around my head.

Is Peter right? Is it just ulcers? Would he really look so ill and wasted? Surely, surely they couldn't let us go on believing that, if it wasn't true? Not now they've got the results of the biopsy? They couldn't be so cruel.

'Lord, I'm so confused. Calm me. Hold me. Help me to hold on to you.'

☆ ☆

'I don't know if this will be any help,' says Chris, the nurse, handing me a sheet of paper. 'But I asked God for a message for you and Peter.'

I take the paper, and begin to read.

'I love you, my children, and I hold your lives securely in my hands.' Tears prick at the back of my eyes, but I read on. 'I will not let either of you fall, nor let you go through anything that you can't cope with. I have my reasons for this trying time. Although they may seem obscure and unseeable now, in the future you will be able to look back and see my hand clearly working in your lives.

'As you look at the blackness before you, be prepared to go through it into the bright sunshine. Have courage, because I am beside you. I have gone before you and I follow behind. My protection is yours.

'I gave my life for you and now you must be prepared to surrender your life and all you possess into my hands. Do not hold anything back and your joy will be great.

'Although you cannot see what lies ahead of you, and your path is strewn with boulders, I hold your hands. I will lead you gently. I know your pain and fears. Trust me. I weep with you and I will laugh with you. I know what I am doing. *I love you.*'

The final words finish me. I — who can never quite believe how anyone could love me, especially God, who knows all about us and sees through all our defences — am a crumpled heap. 'I am at the end of my resources, God. I can only depend on your love. Thank you, oh thank you, for giving it so freely, and to those who deserve it so little.'

When I have wiped my eyes and blown my nose, I type copies for granny and Peter. It doesn't say anything that isn't written many times already in the Bible, but it speaks with power to the centre of our need.

☆　　☆

Peter doesn't say much, but he looks better than he has for months. There is colour in his cheeks. His eyes are brighter. He is almost exuberant. Nobody would believe he was going to have a major operation tomorrow. He is over the moon that something is being done. As far as he is concerned, he is at long last on the way to a cure.

'Darling, don't build your hopes too high,' I pray under my breath.

Before we part, we commit one another into God's keeping, as we do most evenings when the pressure of visitors allows. It is a precious time. Just a couple of sentences, but it is enough. We have always ended the day together in prayer. There is a lot of truth in the statement, 'The family that prays together stays together.' Whatever the tensions of the past twenty-four hours, you have to leave them behind when you come together before God. You either forgive and pray, or you don't pray. It's as simple as that.

Later the priest will be coming to pray and anoint him with oil. He is open to God's blessing. I can leave him in no safer hands.

The bell goes for the end of visiting. The two friends who have been waiting outside rise to come home with me. The hospital doctor in charge of Peter's case is standing by the desk.

'Ah. Mrs Green,' he says. 'You know we're going to operate tomorrow?'

'On what?' I reply.

'Ah . . . Yes . . .' He looks embarrassed. He is tall, fair, angular, and seems incredibly young. 'Has nobody spoken to you?'

I assure him nobody has.

He opens the door to the sister's office.

'Will you come in here, please?'

I signal the friends to stay outside.

Here we go.

'Lord, hold me. Hold me.'

I wonder if the doctor has had to do this before, and what preparation he has had for the task. Precious little I guess, if hospital training is as good as teacher training. In the circumstances he does a remarkably good job. He tells me that the biopsy revealed cancer, but that they will not know until tomorrow how extensive it is. If it is confined, they can operate. If it has spread to other organs, there may be little they can do.

☆      ☆

I sit there, hearing, but not believing. It's as if someone has switched me on to remote control. I feel as if I should be screaming, sobbing, hammering at the windows. In fact I do nothing. I am incapable of a reaction. Something inside me is frozen, paralyzed.

I get up. Go out. I fob off my friends' anxious enquiries, spin them some story. Heaven knows what.

I hear myself answering questions about my work, the

children. Either my cover is holding, or they have sense to let me think so. I go back to the family, still on auto-pilot. Someone is speaking, making the bedtime drinks, registering the phone calls that have accumulated while I have been out.

It isn't me. The real me is a couple of feet away, watching, suspended. Amazed at how my body is performing the expected functions. It seems as though an old cinema reel is running before my eyes, that this cannot really be happening to us. Somehow we have been caught up in the action against our will. If only someone would stop the cameras rolling we could step out of the limelight, and everything would be as normal.

☆    ☆

Operation day. Everyone is on edge. Someone lets Jenny loose with the scissors and glue. I pounce on the two older girls, and the feathers fly. It wasn't their fault, and they let rip back. At least it has cleared the air and relieved some of the tension.

Grandad is next on the hit-list. He passes some comment which I would normally ignore, or deal with relatively calmly. Today I am far from calm. So is everyone else. In my present state I would do best to remove myself from the battle zone, before I say or do something I would regret. I beat a retreat to the library, and stay there till I have simmered down slightly.

Shirley, good friend that she is, comes across in the afternoon. We take ourselves for a walk in the woods. She lets me pour out my anguish and confusion — the anger at the doctors who have let us go on deceiving ourselves, raising our hopes falsely, only to have them dashed twice as low.

Shirley takes it all. I don't know if it's her presence, or the woods, but something soothes my ruffled soul.

☆    ☆

Shirley and Chris come into hospital with me in the evening. Peter is not back from the operating theatre, but we see the young houseman.

'I'm sorry,' he says. 'It's the worst possible. The stomach is stuck down to the aorta. There is nothing we can do.'

☆    ☆

I hear Shirley, Chris, even myself asking questions, the doctor talking about him not being any better than before, of hospices and home nursing services. I feel numbed, but at least we now know the truth. We know what we have to contend with.

'Oh God, I know. Peter doesn't.'

He was so hopeful, so sure that after this operation he was going to be all right. It can't be true. I can't cry.

Afterwards the tears come — outside, in the car, while Shirley goes to tell the priest.

What are we going to tell Peter? We can't tell him what the doctor's told us. We can't take away his hope.

☆    ☆

How can we not tell Peter? Shirley and Len know, the priest knows, Chris knows, the lad who has taken over the leadership of the Nefyn mission has been told.

It is too big a burden to carry alone. They will tell their partners. The partner will need to tell someone else. Already nearly a dozen will have the information. Peter's deputy at school wants to inform the staff. It will be only a matter of time before someone lets it slip, and if everyone knew except Peter he would never forgive us.

They must understand it is to go no further. Not until Peter knows . . . and the children . . . and his parents.

'Lord, his parents. They are waiting to see him get better. What are we going to tell them? What did I tell them last night? That he was still in a side ward, sleeping off the anaesthetic? That he had come through the operation? Some hospital inanity that can cover a multitude of half-truths?

'I don't know. I don't think I lied, but I certainly didn't spell out the full graphic truth. Would they be able to take it?

'And Peter? Lord, what is he to be told? Who is going to tell him? How will he cope?'

56

'No problem,' says one of his colleagues. 'He will handle it.'

I wish I could be so convinced. His track record over the last few months has not been very encouraging. What if he takes it inside himself and sinks into depression? Or locks himself into that inner world of fear and loneliness where it is impossible to reach him? He is a very complex character. Who knows how he will react?

☆　　☆

I discuss the matter with the doctors. They say hospital policy is to spell out the situation only if the patient asks directly, and that Peter is not strong enough yet, that to tell him would be taking away his hope.

'Nonsense,' retorts the priest.'Not if you're a Christian.'

Ah . . . If only it were that easy. Twice I have thought I had cancer. I know the hell of fear it generates. Fear of pain, indignity, death. The possibility of losing life makes everything so much more precious. Unfinished tasks, incomplete relationships, anxiety about those who depend on you.

'Most people have resources inside themselves to cope,' says the ward sister.

Has Peter? He is not good at facing unpleasant realities. He evades and avoids when the going gets tough. It would be incredibly hard to live a lie, for there to be some deception between us, but how will he handle the truth?

☆　　☆

All over the country people who know him are praying for Peter's healing. Now that I have accurate information I know that it would take nothing less than a miracle for him to recover physically. It is possible. God is all-powerful. But would that be the greatest miracle? Would it be right for Peter?

Daily, hundreds have to live with the knowledge that they are terminally ill. We all are. Some of us just reach the end of the journey sooner than others. Would divine intervention be the greatest witness to a world where fear of death holds so many in bondage?

I think maybe the greatest miracle would be if Peter

were given the ability to live with the knowledge most of us spend all our lives trying to avoid.

'Oh, Lord, I don't know. Be with him. Help him. It's so easy when you're the outsider. It's not me it's happening to. If it was it would be a very different kettle of fish.'

☆     ☆

As far as Peter is concerned, he has survived the operation, and is still with us. That is sufficient.

He talks about the nurses, how they are moving him gingerly because they are not sure what was done.

After an eternity I hear myself asking, 'What *was* done?'

'They cut them,' he says. 'Everything's going to be OK.'

He is tearful, apologetic for being there, and I am a coward. I have chickened out of what was maybe Peter's way of asking me to tell him anything I know.

'Lord, I'm so useless. So frightened of hurting people. And I hurt them so much more in the long run by opting out of the painful situations. I know all the excuses. He is weak. I am under stress. There have been so many barriers between us these last few months. Now there is one almighty barrier, and how are we to get over that?'

☆     ☆

Next visiting time Peter is already on the move, staggering down the corridor, holding on to a metal frame with the saline drip attached. I protest, but he is adamant.

'See. You'll be OK,' he says, refusing all offers of help, 'if you do what I say.'

Ha. That one we are going to scotch at birth. It has caused enough trouble already.

'I'm your wife,' I remind him, with a firmness I should have employed months ago, 'not your child. Maybe we would have fewer problems if just occasionally *you* did what *I* say.'

Chris, the nurse, finds it highly amusing.

'That's encouraging,' she says, on the way down in the lift. 'He's walking, and he's putting up a fight.'

☆     ☆

Putting up a fight? He is convinced he is on the way to recovery.

Each day there is another triumph to report. He can take liquids, have a salt bath. The doctors and physiotherapists are pleased with his progress. He can eat solids.

When visitors come, they are treated to a display of his stitches — the most obvious sign that he is 'getting better'. I hear him telling people that it is only a matter of weeks before he will be back at school, laying carpets in the church, standing cheering on the football terraces at West Ham.

I know now how Mary, the mother of Jesus, must have felt as Simeon's prophecy that 'sorrow, like a sharp sword, will break your own heart' began to come true.

☆     ☆

I ask the doctors, again, about telling him.

'Not yet,' they hedge.

The situation is ridiculous. I sense people are beginning to guess as much by what we are not saying as by what is being said. There is no way I can lie about the situation. But neither am I going to share the whole truth until Peter and the family know. It is simply not fair. He has a right to know. He must be told. But how? Who?

'He probably needs to choose his time,' says Len, 'if we are all just open and ready to pick up opportunities. The problem is, he is such a confusing character, it may be never.'

And which of us will have the guts? I don't think anyone relishes the job, any more than I do. There are three vicars and two marriage counsellors, yet we still manage to pass the buck from one to the other for several days.

In the end it is Chris, our curate friend, the one Peter has trained for leadership over a number of years at Nefyn, who sees an opening.

'I feel so much better, physically and spiritually,' Peter informs him. 'If the doctors told me I had only a couple of weeks to live, I could cope.'

Chris takes it from there.

☆ ☆

As soon as he has gone, Peter is on the phone.

'What is this, Chris is saying?' he storms. 'Why haven't I been told?'

☆ ☆

Within ten minutes I am sitting on his bed, explaining how I have been begging for him to be told, but the doctors have kept saying he was not strong enough, and they only tell if the patient asks.

'But I have been asking,' Peter says, with tears in his eyes.

I don't doubt it. But the questions were probably so complex, so obtuse, that only someone with the sensitivity and skill of Chris would have heard them.

☆ ☆

When he has freed himself from his other duties the doctor comes. It is the young hospital doctor. My 'friend'. He ushers us into the comparative privacy of sister's office, and spells out the details to Peter. I am amazed, after all the hedging and half-truths, just how much he tells him.

Peter takes it.

He is very much the headmaster, in full control of the situation. He wants to know what the course of the disease will be, what treatment may be available.

The doctor explains. There is little they can do. Because of the position of the growth, and the nearness of other organs, chemotherapy could do as much harm as good. They can maybe do radiotherapy on his arm, give him more mobility. That is all. If the disease spreads to other organs he may suffer symptoms of jaundice and will probably continue to experience the digestive problems he has already known. Apparently the main discomfort he is likely to face is getting gradually weaker and more tired. The doctor assures Peter that they will be able to control the pain. He talks about the Macmillan home nursing service attached to St Joseph's hospice. The only thing about which he will not commit himself is the subject of time.

'Sometimes these things accelerate, sometimes they slow down,' he says. 'Nobody can really tell. But from the fact that you've had these symptoms for over a year, it would appear that yours is relatively slow-growing.'

Peter thanks him for his information, and the doctor retreats.

As soon as he is out of the door, Peter opens his arms and I nestle into them, regardless of the surgeon's careful handiwork. We need the closeness, the sharing of physical comfort, and the grief. It is a blessing sister has a large box of tissues on her desk.

Peter appears to be hurt, not by the doctor's information, but by the fact that I knew and he didn't. That figures. But at least this way there is one less worry for him to cope with. I have already lived with the knowledge for a week. He is spared the agony of worrying how I would react, and if I should be told.

When the first torrent of tears is past we have a precious time of sharing and prayer. We are very conscious of our heavenly Father holding us as tightly in his arms as we cling to one another. Despite the clashes, the misunderstandings, we have had twenty good years together. With God's help we will make what is left good too. We sang, on our wedding day, a hymn about the God, 'Who from our mother's arms has blessed us on our way, with countless gifts of love.' Deep inside us, and all around is, is the knowledge that he 'still is ours today'. And tomorrow. And next month. Whatever.

We come back to earth with the clatter of tea cups, and sister's loving concern.

I wonder, does she know that God's resources are so much greater than anything we could possibly have inside ourselves?

I have my miracle. As I walk down the hospital steps, I can only thank God, with a mixture of incredulity and relief.

☆     ☆

'People must be told,' Peter insists. 'It's no use one lot getting one story, and others another.'

'What about your mum and dad?' I counter.

Now we know that he is not going to 'get better', but appears so much better, we have suggested it might be time for them to return to Dorset. Understandably, they do not want to go.

'I will talk to them,' he says.

We marshal Shirley to be in the background while Peter gently breaks as much of the news as he, and they, are able to handle.

I gather the three older children in the lounge. I don't know what I say but we all end up in tears. Two arms are just not long enough when you have three children to console.

It hits David hardest, when he realizes that dad will no longer be able to go to football. The parents from school had sent some money for a gift and we had been discussing getting him a season ticket, to cut out the standing. Now even that looks as if it will be out of the question. The message has sunk home.

Mercifully, Margaret has a friend staying the night, as they are off on a school journey tomorrow. Like Peter, she has great difficulty in putting her feelings into words, but it is a mistake to assume that she does not care. She is going to need that friend tonight, and I am very grateful to the mother who is letting her become so much part of our family at the moment.

And what about Debra, the adopted, the chosen one, who has already lost two parents?

I can only wrap her in my arms and talk about the pain her first mum must have suffered when she let her go for adoption, a pain she was prepared to face because she wanted what was best for Deb. Now we can only cling to the knowledge that God knows what is best for dad, however much it may hurt us to let him go.

The tears flow afresh. In the end, because Margaret has her friend and emotions are running high, I suggest Deb comes in with me for the night. She does not need asking twice.

'Lord, it looks as though you're at last beginning to get the message through to me, to whom words are so important, that physical closeness can mean just as much.'

☆　　☆

Granny and grandad are going back to Dorset. I hate the fact that it has to be. I hate myself for enforcing it. The only consolation is that it is for their sakes as much as ours. I don't know how much of what Pete said has really sunk in but I would not like to be responsible for what it could do to them, or him, if they are around to watch their beloved, only son, dying.

It is going to be hard enough a hundred miles away. They cannot be left to cope alone. We must mobilize resources, ask for help, however much it pinches the pride.

Two friends from Peter's home church agree to pop in for a chat, a cup of tea, and the shopping-list.

Pete's pal Ray takes them home and sees that they are safely installed.

Whatever would we do without that second family of ours, the family of God? They are shoring us up on all sides, with practical help, assistance with the children, cuddles, prayer.

Thank God for their prayers. I am not good on my knees. All I can manage is a kind of running dialogue, or occasional agonized yelp. There's such a consciousness of dealing with matters that are beyond our control, a puzzled bemusement as to how it will all work out in the end. There have been so many things to come to terms with, so many things to do.

When I fall into bed, all I am usually capable of is a brief, 'Here I am, Lord. Where do we go now?'

I think we need time, a breathing-space to let it all sink in. Our clergy friends find us details of retreat houses, centres of healing and peace, where dying is not seen as a defeat.

It would be good to be away from the pressures for a while, to let the stillness, the quietness, restore our souls.

I suggest it to Peter, but he only wants to get home. So be it. So would I, in his place. We will see how things go. Play it by ear, as he would say. For one who is nearly tone deaf, and who needs to have everything planned out at least a week in advance if I am not to panic, I am getting quite good at that.

☆     ☆

Pete has had radiotherapy on his shoulder. He is getting more mobility in his arm, but he has cricked his neck because he left off the surgical collar he has been wearing to help with the back pain. He seems tired, depressed.

Is it the new treatment, or a reaction to the emotional and physical upheavals of the last few days? Is the full impact of the conversation with the doctor sinking in?

'Lord, hold him. Give him your peace. There is so little I can do, other than keep handing him over to your keeping.'

☆     ☆

I have had an upset tummy all morning. Ann is bringing my mother to see Pete. It is the first time she will have seen him since we knew there is nothing the doctors can do.

Fortunately Jen and Debra ease the tension of the first few minutes, and in the hospital the nurses are larking around with a water pistol. What with them, and the non-stop verbal cabaret provided by Ann and one of Peter's teaching colleagues, who deserves an Oscar for his performances over the last few weeks, we need not have worried.

It never ceases to amaze me how those who have plumbed the depths in their own lives are often the ones who on the surface appear to have not a care in the world. To hear Ann clowning around you would never think that life appears to have lined up one long series of tragedies, especially for her.

She has picked Peter a basket of spring flowers, primroses and wild daffodils, from the woods of Worcestershire. She teases Peter about being chased by gamekeepers and tearing her knickers on the barbed wire for his sake. It is a happy time. Incredibly.

☆     ☆

Back home the children bound around the house with the scruff of black fur Ann has brought to join our family. Our old dog is going for her final 'walkies'. She is thirteen, and getting very decrepit. She has difficulty climbing the stairs.

I have seen the expression on Peter's face as he watched her. It did not require a degree in psychology to know what was going on in his mind. Not on that issue, anyway.

She has to go. But the children will miss her. They need something to divert their attention. The last few months have not been easy, and they are certainly not going to get any brighter in the immediate future.

Shirley thinks I am mad to take on another dog, particularly a puppy, at such a time. I disagree. Life is becoming too fraught. We need a little light relief. It looks as though we've got it.

'Scamp. Scamp,' the youngsters scream, as they tumble over chairs and tables in hot pursuit of the pup.

Now we have two scamps in the family. One on four legs, and one on two who is nearly four years old. I watch them romping together.

Oh, Jenny. My poor little one. The apple of daddy's eye. You're so like him. The broad shoulders, thick lips, the sharp brain, the determination. How can we prepare you for what is to come? How do you tell a three-year-old that the daddy she loves so much is not going to 'get better', even when she has a new puppy to help ease the pain?

☆　　☆

Just before they release Peter from hospital he has three special visitors. We gave up keeping our running total of professionals when we got overtaken by weightier concerns. Whoever came, they were welcome, but none more so than these three lads, former pupils, who brave hospital authorities, a posse of visiting headteachers, and the sight of their former authority-figure in a pair of over-size pyjamas and a surgical collar.

The fact that the leader was the lad Peter had to discipline probably more times than any other child in the school astounds everybody, including Peter. He couldn't have had a better present, if those boys had come gift-wrapped.

☆     ☆

Peter is home. He is once more part of the family.

Jenny is delighted. She thrives on the visitors, the busyness, being able to do things for Peter. I have not spelt out all the implications of his illness to her, but neither am I filling her with false promises. As far as she is concerned, although he is not 'getting better' in the sense that we all hoped, she is helping to look after him.

Whether her ministrations are always appreciated is a different matter. The energy, and sheer volume, of a three-year-old is exhausting at the best of times. When you yourself lack strength even to concentrate on a news item in the paper, or to haul yourself out of the chair for a trip to the toilet, the frustrations must be enormous. Fortunately the weather is getting warmer and our house is fairly large, so it is not too difficult to occupy her out of earshot, when Peter has had enough.

Knowing when he has reached that limit, or getting him to acknowledge it, is a tougher task. The day before he came out of hospital he had twenty-six visitors. At least, at home, we can try to space them a little. If only people would stick to the ten minutes or half-hour they mentioned on the telephone. They never do. Peter can be sitting in the chair, experiencing great difficulty in keeping his eyes open, and still they chatter on. Then the doorbell rings, and the next visitor is ushered in, and Pete rallies his resources for the next session.

It's different with the specials — the old friends who have meant so much.

His college friend comes to see him. It is as if the twenty years since we were all training to be teachers did not exist. The conversation may now be about falling numbers, staff–pupil relationships, and new initiatives in education, rather than rag processions and rugger matches: the feeling of being comfortable with someone with whom you have shared an important chunk of your life has not altered.

Neither has Peter's determination.

It is Margaret's birthday. She wants a camera, and Peter has made up his mind that he is going with her to get it.

'You can drop me outside the shop,' he says, 'and we'll have a look around. Then we'll just pop across to Woolworths and Argos to compare prices.'

It is useless trying to argue. I can only pray that someone will know what to do if he collapses in the street, and that it won't give the children too much of a fright.

Trying to get him to eat anything nutritious is another source of tension. I pore through the recipe books for things that look tempting. If he seems interested in the eventual product, you can guarantee that the phone will ring, someone will call, or he will need to disappear to the toilet for the next half-hour. His staple diet seems to be ice-cream, mousse, and *langues de chat* biscuits. The dog is the one who usually ends up with the fillets of plaice and sirloin steak.

☆       ☆

The children pack their bags for the Easter holidays. Four lively youngsters bounding around the place all day, every day, would be just too much for Peter. Jenny is going to my mother for a bit of spoiling, the big ones are off to the Lake District and Scottish border country with a friend. Deb sneaks off to aunty Ann at the first possible opportunity. They are kindred spirits, fun-loving, extrovert, never afraid to express their feelings. They will do one another a power of good.

Before they go, we share the shiny Easter egg they bought for Peter when he was in hospital. Jen has had her eyes on it ever since she first saw it. Now they can sink their teeth into it as well.

☆       ☆

A series of postcards keeps us up-to-date with their progress around the country. David and Margaret lose one another in a supermarket in Blackpool; sleep on the gear-stick of the car at Gretna Green; are overwhelmed by the splendours of Edinburgh.

Debra spends most of her time out in the stock wagon with Ann's fiancé. She is revelling in sheep dips, pub lunches, and the rough and tumble of life with ten ferrets, three dogs, a cat, and two adolescent boys. The little girl doesn't get much of a mention. I think Deb has enough hassle with the one back home.

Not to be outdone, Jenny is organizing my aunt into playing nursery schools every morning and, every afternoon, getting slightly less of her own way with the little girl who lives next door to my mother.

Good. They are well and happy. Only a yearning creeps into the end of their letters. 'Hope dad's feeling better.'

☆　　　☆

Easter Sunday. Resurrection. Hm. Peter is at home, talking with the union rep. It would be too much for him to sit through a two-hour service. We have shared 'This is the Day' on the television earlier. It has become a Sunday ritual: lighting the candle for the good news of the gospel, breaking bread together, sharing the fellowship of the suffering of God's people in situations far worse than our own.

'Give us peace, courage and bright hope, today and all our days,' was the blessing at the end of that service.

'Please, Lord, this Easter is so different to the one I imagined — I need your strength, your love . . . for Peter, to be able to let him go.'

Tears blur my eyes. I know that a special awareness of God's presence is unlikely. The worship area is in the final throes of reorganization. They are laying the carpet Peter thought he would be doing. We are meeting in the playgroup hall. None of us knows quite where, or how, to stand, as we move forward to receive the bread and wine. There is a crush of bodies, children made restless by the change in routine, little of the space and stillness I would normally associate with the reaching out of my faltering spirit to an appreciation of the nearness of the Almighty. It is perhaps just as well. I don't know that I could cope with it.

Suddenly, it is as if the shutters of my limited sight are

pulled back, as though Jesus is physically present, saying my name.

'Wendy. I love you. Do you need anything more?'

I know that the response I have been conditioned to give should be 'no'. That to say anything different would be an admission of spiritual failure. It would also be dishonest. I have to answer 'Yes'.

It is as though a great load is rolling from my mind. It is all right to say that. It is safe. God won't reject me because of it. He made me. He knows me . . . oh . . . so much better than I have known myself all these years. He knows I need people. He knows how I need to be loved, even though I have found it so hard to admit. There is no contradiction. He made us, body and spirit, capable of loving and receiving love, human and divine. His love is always there. I know, like St Paul, I could not exist apart from that. In him I live, and move, and have my being. The lesson I still have to learn is that he loves me . . . as I am. Which, at the moment, is very much in need of all the strength and support I can get. What it will mean for the future, I have yet to discover.

☆ ☆

We have time. We have space. We are together. Yes, there are still people. But not so many. Lots are out of town over Easter, or have the sense to give us a bit of a break. The children are still away. There are fewer household pressures. We can eat when we feel like it, ignore routine. Just be. Relax. Find peace and strength in one another, and in God. Going on a retreat has not been possible. The journey home from hospital made that obvious, and Pete is content just to be at home. Having this space is sufficient. It is as if we have retreated from the world. God is very present. Healing.

'The healing will come through relationships,' prophesied a wise woman. It feels as though it is.

☆ ☆

'What shall we pray?' agonizes a friend 200 miles away, who cannot see the miracles unfolding before our eyes.

'That we should take a day at a time,' says Peter.

Amen to that. To think of next week, next month, could blow our minds.

Sorting out the summer holidays is bad enough. The 'holiday of a lifetime' in France is out of the question. It has to be cancelled. Could we go to Nefyn, book some isolated cottage in the country, where Peter and I can just sit in the sun and chat with friends, while the children join in the fun on the beach? For a while it seems possible, but as the days pass it appears less likely. Nefyn is 250 miles away, right across country, on the furthest tip of Wales. It would be too much to ask of Peter's weakening body.

Whatever happens, the children must have their holiday and as much normality as possible. We must make arrangements that are not dependent on us. The doctors may not commit themselves about time, and Peter is still talking in terms of four years, even forty. I think he will be lucky to make it to the end of the summer.

☆      ☆

'It hasn't sunk in,' I agonize to Shirley. 'He's still talking about going back to school, things he is going to be doing in the future.'

'What do the Macmillan people say?' she asks. 'Have you asked them?'

I haven't, but I do. To know that you can pick up the phone and ask to speak to someone is a terrific strength. Such problems are not too trivial for them, and you get, not superficial answers, but the skill and expertise of years of experience.

You know where you stand with them. They don't come in waving sheets of prescriptions, advising 'swallow this, and you'll be all right.' They listen to what you need. It is nothing for them to spend an hour with Pete, identifying where he is at, gently easing out of him what the doctors have said, helping him to face reality.

Helping me, too.

'I think you should be thinking in terms of weeks rather than months,' the sister says, after one visit.

'Lord, so soon? So inevitable? If I find that hard to

accept, no wonder Pete is blocking it with half his mind. So would I be. Have been, Lord. Forgive me. Help him.'

The water-works are in full flood again. It is a wet week all round.

☆     ☆

Peter is talking to a visitor about the Macmillan service.

'What is it?' the visitor enquires.

'A home nursing service,' Peter says. He pauses. There is a catch in his voice. 'For the terminally ill.'

Oh, Pete. My love, It's so hard to believe. What must it be like for you?

☆     ☆

A magazine plops through the letter-box. Pete leafs through it. It contains news of children's missions, holiday activities, people we know. I carry on with my work. Pete passes the magazine to me. He doesn't say anything but his thumb points to an article. I read that a friend's father has had a heart attack, and Peter Green has cancer of the stomach, which has proved to be inoperable.

I fob it off with some inane comment about the friend's father, then wrap myself round Pete's knees and burst into tears.

'It looks so stark in print,' I wail.

Pete tries to soothe me.

'Don't be silly,' he says.

'I'm not being silly,' I sob. 'Just normal.'

☆     ☆

'Lord . . . your help . . . your wisdom . . . to handle all these emotions. Please. I'm so bad at it. There's so many years' backlog of denying my feelings, burying them deep inside, tying myself in knots. Help me to stop devaluing my humanity, blanking myself off from feeling. My husband is dying. It hurts. It hurts to watch the humilities he has to endure. It hurts to let go. It's no use denying it, no use pretending. That would be no good to me, no good to him, and catastrophic for the kids. They are going to

71

need freedom to express their feelings, their fears. There must be no dissembling. We all need to know how much we mean to one another.'

☆     ☆

'Dad doesn't make it sound half as serious as you do,' says David one day, when they have all returned home for the start of the summer term.

I try to explain how he has had less time to adjust, to let it sink in, how our minds play tricks with the things they find hard to believe.

I don't want to take away their hope, to sink them in doom and gloom, but if they are living on false hope it will only be harder for them in the long-term.

☆     ☆

'We can control the pain,' said the young hospital doctor. 'But what you will experience is gradually feeling more tired, weaker.'

'Lord, it's happening before our eyes. First it was the bath. He did so love a bath, Lord. Now it's the stairs, the telephone, getting out of the armchair, going to the loo. Lord, he spends hours in the toilet.'

I think of the publicity poster we used one year at Nefyn. A child shouting 'Let's get going,' and rushing off to some activity. Pete found it highly amusing, cracked a variety of jokes about prunes and such like, and stuck a copy in the downstairs loo.

'It's not funny any longer, Lord. I've always joked about my side of the family coming to a quick end, with a history of heart illnesses on both sides. For that may I be eternally grateful. I think I would prefer it to the slow indignities of what the florist rightly calls 'this disgusting disease'.'

☆     ☆

We are reading Psalms. Just two or three verses each evening. According to the Bible-reading scheme we use, we should be studying Ezekiel, but that is beyond me at the best of times. Now it is beyond Peter too. Psalms are more our wavelength. The psalmists have walked where we are.

They knew the heights, and the depths:

'From the depths I call to you,
Lord, listen to my cry for help,'

pleads Psalm 130. Pete wants to hear that, and the following one, over and over again. Rely on God. Rely on God. Rely on God, hammers the message. How can we do anything else? Only he can do anything.

The doctors may have the physical pain under control, but to me the real miracle is taking place in Peter's mind.

'My heart has no lofty ambitions,
my eyes do not look too high,'

says Psalm 131.

'I am not concerned with great affairs
or marvels beyond my scope.'

Peter has had education officers taking school lunch duty in the middle of a teachers' union walk out, and represented all the headteachers of the Inner London Education Authority in liaisons with County Hall. Now it is as much as he can do to put his slippers on. He could be bitter, resentful, frustrated, angry. He is not. The psalm continues, 'Enough for me to keep my soul tranquil and quiet, like a child in its mother's arms.'

That is where he is. Back where he began. An only child, born late in his parents' life. Very loved. Very precious. But the arms he is snuggling in now are those that cradle the universe.

'I am happy,' he tells his visitors.

He is. People come to commiserate, and go away strengthened.

Some want to pray for physical healing. Peter talks rather of wholeness, the healing that comes from knowing yourself safe in God's love, the knowledge that he is in control. Whatever.

'I will heal him. I will indeed heal him,' promised a verse of scripture, when I was reading and praying one day.

'Lord, I can see you honouring that promise. If Peter is at peace with you, that is the greatest healing any of us can know. I am content to leave him in your hands.'

☆      ☆

We listen to preacher and evangelist David Watson on the radio, talking about how he believes God is healing him physically from cancer. Afterwards I am supposed to be collecting Margaret from her friend's house, but I sit in the car and howl my eyes out, instead.

'Lord, is it lack of faith . . . that we're not pushing physical healing? Fear that you can't do it? How can it be? I believe you are the God of time and space. The knowledge we are beginning to explore in the fields of lasers and micro-surgery, you have at your finger-tips. You have only to snap your fingers and Peter would be healed.

'Is it something in me, then? Maybe I don't want Peter well? Do I see this as the easy way out of the emotional hassles of the last year? It has to be considered. Seriously. And discounted. I know too much about single parent-hood to walk willingly into sole responsibility for the children, the financial hazards, worries about the house — and the agony of loss that aches through one of my favourite records, Cliff Richard singing 'Miss you, nights'. We may have our conflicts, our misunderstandings. We also have the strength of our love for one another, and for you.

'So, what do you want? Should we apply pressure for the spectacular, the miraculous, what *we* want? Or do we hold on to you and know that however far down we go, you are there?'

I begin to pray about physical healing. For the third time. And for the third time it is as if God is saying, 'Hang on. Wait. That may not be what I have in mind.'

The Bible verse, 'If a grain of wheat falls into the ground and dies it will bear much fruit,' echoes in my ears.

It is not a threat, but a promise.

'Oh, Lord. You're doing it again. That's not the one I wanted to hear.'

☆      ☆

'He's doing OK,' Shirley says when I howl it all out on her shoulder. 'He believes that he could get better, but he knows, if it's the worst, God is with him. He'll handle the ups and downs in between.'

☆　　☆

Peter is holding on to the washbasin, steadying himself while he cleans his teeth. The next move will be to sit on the bathroom stool while I wash his swollen feet. It is the least I can do to compensate for his not being able to have a bath.

'I think you're incredible,' I say. 'The way you're coping.'

He gestures the idea away, impatiently.

'You should have known I would,' he says.

I think of the hassles with dad, the agonies I saw behind the scenes with the relatives of the other patients in Peter's ward. I shake my head.

'No,' I argue. 'That's the problem. Nobody knows.'

☆　　☆

We debate whether to buy Peter a colour television. The children have been petitioning for one for years, but there has never been any spare money for non-essentials. In this kind of situation it doesn't seem such a luxury. Maybe we could use the money we would have spent on France?

Before we can get to the shops, the doorbell rings. A man is standing outside.

'Colour television,' he says.

'No,' I reply.

'Yes. For Green,' he insists.

'But we haven't ordered one.'

'Ah. There's something about that,' he mutters. 'In an envelope. On top of it.'

He wheels an enormous box to the doorstep. A note explains that it is a gift from Peter's fellow headteachers.

'But why?' Peter says, through his tears. 'Why have they done this?'

'Just a token of our thanks for all you have done,' says Doreen, the friend who organized the collection, when she calls in later. 'And there's a small cheque too.'

She winks at me. The small cheque is for £600.

☆　　☆

The next week Doreen is on the receiving end. Her husband Rod has to go into hospital for major surgery. The person she most wants to be with is Peter.

'He's always been like a big brother to me,' she explains.

He has to a great many. Maybe that's the secret of all the love that is being showered upon him now?

He is still giving out, still refusing to give in. He stays up till all hours, watching snooker on the colour telly. I am desperate for sleep but I cannot leave him to climb the stairs alone, and would never rest till he was in bed, in any case. I make the mistake of mentioning that the automatic tea-maker is not working properly when he has got as far as the bathroom, just before midnight one night. I expect him to look at it the next day, poke a wire through the spout or something. He has to deal with it then and there, taking the whole unit apart, fumbling with minute screws my fingers would not be able to manipulate at the best of times. Watching his determination not to be beaten, I don't know whether to laugh or cry.

☆  ☆

The vicar comes to give Peter communion. He talks about the church accounts, a youth club for punk rockers, the alterations which are now nearing completion, Peter's health. Pete makes light of that last subject.

'Even the doctors don't know what it is, do they Wendy?' he says.

'Help,' I gulp at God. 'What do I say now?'

'Darling, they've told you what it is,' I say. I know they have. I was there with him. He said people should know.

'What do they say?' he persists.

I take a deep breath. There is no way out.

'Cancer of the stomach,' I reply.

We need that communion service. Badly.

☆  ☆

The following Tuesday Peter has to visit outpatients. It is six weeks since he was discharged from hospital. All the appointments are running late. There has been an emergency. We can make another appointment and go home, or we can wait. We wait. All that effort getting dressed, into the car, hanging around? Go through it again? No thank you.

Peter sits in a wheelchair. It is more comfortable than the normal seats.

Two other former patients from his ward are also waiting. It is the first time one of them has been out since he was in hospital. He lives alone, three floors up in a block of flats. A male friend pops in occasionally to see how he is. The other one is in a bad way. He can't eat, has frequent vomiting attacks, and his wife is beside herself with worry.

'Nobody seems to care,' she wails. 'We never see the same doctor twice. The district nurse has called in a couple of times. He's worse than before he went into hospital. What do they expect you to do?'

I think of all the support we are getting, and grieve for the lonely, the bewildered. But what can I do? Peter is sitting in the wheelchair, waiting, a fixed smile on his face.

I can only pat her hand, and shake my head.

I must rejoin Peter. Be there, for him. Ensure he is not alone.

☆       ☆

He has two questions for the specialist.

'Wendy uses the word cancer. In all our conversations you have never used that term. What is the matter with me?'

The specialist mumbles about lesions, malignancy, abnormal growth, the terms being interchangeable.

The second question is equally direct.

'Are my back problems related to the growth?'

'I don't like to be dogmatic,' says the specialist. 'But in your case it looks as though they are.'

He talks about pressure on the spinal column, draws diagrams on the piece of paper where Peter has written his queries.

'The main problem now,' he explains, 'is self starvation. Because of the stomach's smaller capacity you must educate yourself to eat small amounts, often. Instead of three main meals a day, break it down into five or six.'

We come away almost reassured. There is something positive we can do. The specialist was so calm, so confident. We have booked another appointment for six weeks' time.

When we get home, Peter relays the information to the children. It all sounds so sane, so comforting.

It is only later the enormity of it sinks in.

'Oh, God. It's appalling. Horrible.'

Peter. Peter. Peter.

☆　　　☆

On Wednesday our previous minister comes down from the Midlands to see Peter. They talk about the church, and all the alterations that have taken place.

'I haven't seen it since it was finished,' says Peter wistfully.

'Why don't you take Alan round?' I suggest. 'You have the keys.'

They go in Alan's car, but there is no mistaking who is taking whom. There is a smile of satisfaction on Peter's face when he returns. It is another job well done.

☆　　　☆

On Thursday it is as much as Peter can do to get dressed and sit in the chair. I blame myself. That trip to church was too much after the visit to outpatients.

But it was worth it for the look on his face.

In the evening, when things have calmed down slightly after the usual flow of visitors, Peter calls me to him. He wants to initiate me into the intricacies of rates and car insurance. It is as clear as mud, but I dare not admit it, dare not think of why he should now consider it necessary. I must force myself to concentrate and ask him about transferring to a joint account. Friends are horrified that we do not already have one and, knowing all the headaches it could create, I suggest the possibility to Peter.

'Whatever for?' he demands. 'Our system has always worked all right so far, hasn't it? Why do you want to change it now?'

☆　　　☆

On Friday he has pains in his chest. I ring the sister at the

78

hospice. She has a long chat with him at lunchtime.

'I'm so confused,' he says. 'The doctors at the hospital imply one thing, and you another.'

'Then you're going to have to choose which of us to believe, aren't you?' she replies gently.

When she has left, I go in to him. He is sitting in the armchair in the corner, surrounded by my jungle of plants, and all the pots and baskets of flowers people have brought for him — as he is in the photo Margaret has taken of him with her new camera.

He holds out his hand to me.

'If I go home to Jesus, what will you do?' he asks.

I burst into tears and cuddle against him. Through the sniffles, I manage to say, 'Miss you, nights'.

The tears flow again, from both of us.

When we are calmer, I remind him of the reverse side of the coin. How the Lord is our shepherd — his and mine, and David's and Margaret's and Debra's and Jenny's. How he is looking after all of us, and will honour all that Peter has done and been, to draw others into a knowledge of his love.

I don't know where the words are coming from. Certainly from no coherent pattern in my brain. Another bit of God's incredible by-pass surgery?

'But what about you?' I wail. 'Life is so good, and we don't appreciate it, till we're threatened by the loss of it.'

I talk about how I felt the two times I thought I had cancer. How everything became sharpened up, so much more precious.

On the coffee table there is a basket of flowers from school. They are vibrant with life, beauty.

'And God saw everything that he had made,' says the first chapter of Genesis, 'and, behold, it was very good.'

It is good. So good. Wouldn't it be an insult to the Creator if we were not sad to leave it, however much we may have to gain?

I share my thoughts.

Pete presses my hand and nods assent. It is enough. We have stood in each other's shoes. We understand the battles each is facing. We are not fighting them alone.

Later that afternoon I suggest bringing the bed settee out of the spare room, so that he can sleep downstairs. It is agony watching him postponing the evil hour when he has to summon every reserve of energy to climb the stairs. Show jumping, snooker, late-night chat shows, any excuse is sufficient.

I expect a fight but there is none.

That night he is in bed shortly after 9 p.m.

☆    ☆

Next day he has a turn for the worse. He looks awful. In the evening I think he is going to die. I phone my mother.

'It's all right,' she says. 'I'm coming. I'll be with you by lunchtime tomorrow.'

☆    ☆

Chris, the nurse, collects her from the coach station. I know what it must be costing her to come into this situation, but mum is running true to form. Something difficult to handle? Shoulders back, chin out, let's get on with it, meet it head on.

'How are you, Peter Geeky,' she says, loving him with the easy affection that comes so naturally to her.

'Hello, Marge,' he says, holding her hand and focusing a smile.

A couple of minutes are enough. She must not push herself further. The pain of last year is still too raw. Not for the first time, I thank God that she was spared watching my father die. Even when my granny died, she was out for the afternoon. More than ten years' nursing, constant care, pushing her around in a wheelchair, and at the end it was my auntie and the teenage version of myself who found ourselves sitting with my grandmother while she talked about the beautiful city she could see, and the last breaths rattled in her throat.

Hey-ho. The Bible says that 'all things work together for good, for those who love God'. Little did I know then how much I was going to need that experience.

☆    ☆

'One thing, your children are never going to be afraid of death,' says the nursing sister.

I don't know that I agree with her. Peter is not in pain, but it is incredibly painful to watch.

'Is there any chance of him going back into hospital?' I enquire.

'Have you discussed it with Mr Green?' she asks.

Have I *what*? She just has to be joking.

'We'll send in a night nurse,' she compromises. 'Then at least you'll get some sleep.'

☆　　☆

Monday, Bank Holiday, May Day.

'Would you like us to come across and share communion together?' Len asks on the telephone. 'With the whole family?'

Would you like it Peter? He would.

It is as much as he can do to move, or sit up. He doesn't want to eat, but he is still mentally alert.

By the time Len and Shirley have driven over from Romford, our college friend, Janet, has arrived from the Midlands. She's another one who thinks of Peter as a big brother, and is semi-official aunt and godmother to our four children.

We sit in a circle in the lounge, Pete propped up on pillows, while Len administers communion. Another piece of God's incredible manoeuvring.

It is the only day Janet is free in weeks. That she and Shirley and Len, who have volunteered to act as joint guardians for the children, should be able to share with us at such a time and in such a way, is a great source of strength.

Shirley has come prepared. She has a bag of goodies ready, to occupy Jenny's attention. With three children of her own she knows there is no way a three-year-old is going to sit silent through a service of communion — however up-to-date and abbreviated — especially one as articulate as Jenny.

☆　　☆

Jenny comes into the room while I am sitting with Peter later that afternoon. She looks at him. Her eyes widen. I know what is going on in her mind. Long before all this happened, she censored out of her bookcases anything with a wolf, witch, ogre, giant, anything nightmarish or uncomfortable.

I take her upstairs and sit her on my lap.

'Lord, the right words. Please.'

'Daddy is very poorly,' I explain.

She nods her head.

'He isn't going to get any better.'

Gulp.

'It's hard for us to look at him, isn't it?'

Another nod.

'Shall we ask Jesus to take him where he will look after him, and there's no more sickness, or sorrow, or pain?'

'Yes.' She snuggles against me. We pray.

'Oh, Lord, you hear the prayer of this little one. And her mother, too.'

☆     ☆

One of the doctors looks in. There is little she can do.

'A couple of days,' she says.

'God, it's still so hard to believe. There's been so little time for it to sink in. And what about the children? If I can't grasp it, how much have they taken in? Do they need the warning too?'

I wait until Jenny is in bed and the older ones are together.

The doctor says it may only be a couple of days,' I explain.

Deb bursts into tears, and flings her arms round my mother.

'I didn't think it would be so soon,' she sobs.

Neither did any of us.

☆     ☆

Peter dozes in the corner. The children are sitting in a row on the couch on the other side of the room, watching 'Coronation Street', with Margaret's friend. I would never have dreamed it possible. My brood might not have much option. But the friend is here by choice.

☆ ☆

Tuesday, Peter does not take anything, except sips of water or tea.

He cannot even swallow the tablets he would normally take. But he is not in pain.

His mother wants to come from Dorset, I don't think it is a good idea. Neither do the folk who are with her, though they are prepared to bring her if that is what she wants. In the end she decides to stay, and we all breathe a sigh of relief. It is better she remembers the Peter she said goodbye to in the hospital.

☆ ☆

David comes in from school, asks, 'How's dad?', takes one look at him, and goes and kicks the dog and the football round the garden for half an hour.

☆ ☆

Wednesday morning, my alarm is set for 5.30 a.m. I have to take over when the night nurse goes off duty. I open the curtains. The sycamore tree at the bottom of the garden is in full leaf. It must have been budding, gradually unfurling, turning into leaf, for a month or more. I have not been conscious of the fact. I check the other trees in the neighbourhood. There are at least five visible from the window. They are all in varying degrees of leaf and bud. None of them is in full leaf. I swallow hard, and go downstairs.

The nurse is brisk and business-like. Peter has had a restless night, but he is now sleeping peacefully. I thank her and let her out through the front door. In the front garden, which usually displays an assorted collection of crisp bags and sweet-papers from the school next door, irises and tulips glow with an early morning clarity I am not often around to see. That 'other world' seems almost as real and vivid and close. It stays that way through all the bustle of children getting ready for school, doctors and nurses, people coming and going.

83

The doctor tries to turn Peter. He is obviously not used to doing it, and I am not much help.

'Sister doesn't usually do it that way,' Peter informs him. He explains how he should be doing it.

'He's a headmaster,' I apologized. 'He's used to telling people what to do.' The doctor doesn't seem to mind. He bends over him.

'I'll just explain what I'm going to do with this medication,' he says.

'You don't need to,' Peter replies. 'I heard you telling Wendy.'

☆　　☆

The sister comes. She persuades Peter to eat some ice-cream.

'Is there anything else we can give him?' I ask.

'What about some jelly?' she suggests. 'That slips down easily.'

Jenny helps me to make it. She seems less bothered about being with Peter since our talk on Monday, and loves doing things for him. She eats her evening meal in the lounge, when the children's programmes have finished on the television, then trots out to help my mother in the kitchen.

I ask Peter if he wants anything to eat, and he decides he will try some jelly. He opens his mouth for a spoonful, then focuses his eye directly on mine.

'If I eat this it means I'm getting better, doesn't it,' he says, and shuts his mouth.

'Jenny made this for you,' I reply.

He eats two spoonfuls.

☆　　☆

It is nearly 7 p.m. Outside, the sky is grey, but the clouds part slightly to let out a shaft of silver light. I look at Peter.

'It's getting brighter,' I say.

He smiles.

'What have you got to smile about?' I tease.

☆　　☆

Two of the Welsh girls on the mission team have sent Debra a tape of themselves singing. Peter wants to hear it. Most of the songs are in Welsh but there is one in English, 'Sing unto the Lord a new song.'

Peter listens, then signals for it to be switched off. He wants to know the date and the time. I think he is confused, that the tape has distressed him and he thinks he should be getting ready for the Nefyn mission.

'We must do this properly,' he says, in speech now slurred by weakness. 'When my hand goes up, put the tape on; when it goes down, switch it off.'

I do as I am told.

Often I cannot understand what he is saying. It is a source of frustration to us both. I know the effort it will involve for him to repeat his words. He thinks I am not listening. Fair enough. I would rather he believed that.

I ask if he wants the children, but he just wants to 'be quiet with God'. He asks for Psalms 130 and 131. We say the Lord's Prayer. Several times. He lies with his arms outstretched, willing himself into that other world which is now so close, even I feel that if I stretch out my hand I will surely reach into it. When his physical symptoms bring him back to reality he sighs, as if to say, 'Am I still here?'

☆       ☆

Upstairs I can hear Jenny crying as she is put to bed.

'I want my mummy. I want my mummy.'

Tonight Peter's need is greater. She will have me far longer than he now has.

☆       ☆

The doorbell rings. Shirley and Len arrive. They said they would come tonight. I meant to tell them not to worry, that all was in order. But I forgot — thank the Lord.

Mother pokes her head round the door, but I signal her away.

Shirley and Len will understand. They will have enough to do, being there for mum and the children.

☆        ☆

Peter clasps my hand. His is cold and clammy.

'I love you,' he says.

I place my other hand over his.

'And I love you,' I reply.

I can say it. I can mean it. It is not just hollow words.

Peter's other hand completes the pyramid.

'Let there be new beginnings,' he pronounces.

Oh, my love. I don't think we have any choice.

☆        ☆

Peter is restless. It is half-past eight. He wants to be moving. The light is fading.

'Come on, then. Let's get going,' he says suddenly, in his normal voice.

'It isn't time yet,' I soothe.

Lesser beings, intimidated by his organizational ability, know that if everyone and everything is not ready at least half an hour before the event, they are in trouble. God works to his own time-scale. Peter has met his match. Even so, he is only ten minutes ahead of schedule. At ten-past nine I can walk no further with him. He is home. Healed. Perfect. Complete.

☆        ☆

I switch into a burst of hyperactivity. I must be doing, tidying, on the move. I am angry. Not with God, but with Satan, who keeps us bound all our lives by fear of death.

'OK, you,' I rail at him. 'You've done your worst. And Peter has won through. You can't get him any more.'

I roll up my sleeves, and swish disinfectant into a bucket in a fury. The words of a poem I learned in school echo in my head:

'Death, be not proud, though some have called thee

Mighty and dreadful for thou art not so . . .'

The poet was right. Our fears are based on a lie, perpetrated by the father of all lies. God is able to hold his children, take them through to new beginnings. Peter can sing his new song. So shall I. The confidence we can have . . . that comes, not from ourselves, but from our God. I am on the offensive, going out to do battle. Peter's is over. Mine may be only just beginning.

☆　　　☆

Len stands looking down at Peter.

'Pete, old mate,' he says softly. 'I don't understand this. I doubt if I ever shall. But somehow this is right.'

☆　　　☆

When the practicalities have been dealt with, and Shirley and Len have returned to their own family I take a deep breath and go to see how the children are faring. Jenny, miraculously, has slept through all the comings and goings. David and Margaret are red-eyed, but coping. Debra huddles against my mother.

'I can't cry,' she says bleakly.

I know the feeling.

'It's OK, love,' I try to assure her. 'It's shock. You will. Some minor little thing will trigger it off. So watch out.'

She smiles, wryly. Mum gives her a hug. Ginger head against the black.

Thank God for families — with all their faults and failures.

☆　　　☆

We sleep, No bad dreams tonight. It is over. There is nothing else we can do.

☆　　　☆

In the morning, Jenny creeps into my bed, as she does every morning.

Oh. 'This is going to be the hardest task, Lord. The words. What do I say?'

There is a card beside the tea-maker, covered in butterflies. It arrived yesterday.

'Jenny.'

She is alert. Listening. Like Peter. Bright as a button. Out of bed and into action. Another source of tension. It takes me half an hour to get mobile, and then only reluctantly. That's why we had the tea-maker. To give me some form of incentive to get moving.

I try to focus my thoughts, wrench them back to the present.

Jenny is waiting. I hug her to me.

'You know we prayed that prayer the other day — asked God to take daddy to be safe with him?'

She nods, silent for once.

'Well, during the night God answered that prayer. Daddy has gone to be with him, where there is no more sorrow, or pain.'

Margaret has crept into the room. She snuggles in beside us. I pick up the card.

'Look at the butterflies,' I say. 'Remember the story of the very hungry caterpillar?'

As if anyone could forget it? The bright pictures, delightful tale — of the caterpillar who stuffed himself for a week, had a stomachache, went to sleep, and woke to find himself changed into a beautiful butterfly.

Jenny remembers.

'That's a bit like what's happened to daddy.'

I fumble for the right words, fearful she will have a mental picture of Peter complete with butterfly wings, doing aerobics in his new-found freedom.

There are a few questions. Not many. There is no need. It has happened before. You can almost see her mind clicking it through.

One day grandad was there, the next he wasn't. This is one more painful fact to be assimilated. Now it is time for breakfast!

There are no tears. Well, not from her anyway. Margaret and I are a bit damp around the eyeballs.

☆    ☆

We give the older ones the choice of whether they want to go to school, and face their friends. Margaret and David want to get it over. Deb is not ready yet. Jenny doesn't get any option. She needs the routine. We need the space.

I phone the secondary school to warn them, but tell the nursery teacher in front of Jenny. Now she has freedom to know she can talk about it, and the teacher has some preparation for when she does.

☆    ☆

Back home, the phone is ringing. Shirley and Len are coming over. As if they haven't done enough. They are the ones who got landed with all the unpleasantries last night, bless them. It cannot have been easy. Now they are coming to help sort out the rest of the practicalities.

No false offers, hoping I will refuse. No mention of the thousand-and-one jobs they will be leaving in their own parish. No possibility of argument. Just a plain statement of fact. The assessment of a need.

And how? I wouldn't know where to start, even though we've been through the process three times over, in recent years.

Mum finds in Shirley a kindred spirit. By the time Len and I have marshalled the necessary documents, they have evicted most of the furniture from the lounge, and are starting on a marathon spring clean. Fine. It will do mum a power of good. Release some of that pent-up energy. Deb looks less enthusiastic. She has been conned into cleaning the windows. I have a sneaking suspicion she will be opting to go back to school after lunch.

☆          ☆

Len is just what I need. His gentle presence pilots me through the maze of bureaucracies that accompany modern living, and dying.

Fill in this. Sign here. Date. Time. Details. Certificates. It is all so cold-blooded. Thank God I am still in a semi-daze, not really registering.

Only when I hold the death certificate in my hands does it really hit through.

Cause of death: carcinoma of the upper half of the stomach.

Oh, Peter. I don't believe it. Don't want to believe it.

I wish I could tear it into a thousand shreds.

Oh, my love. Why did you go and do it?

☆          ☆

We stop at a garage. The car needs air in the tyres. It has done for several months. I am useless with anything mechanical, especially if it hisses and frightens you into thinking you are doing more harm than good.

'Make me do it,' I instruct Len. 'Don't do it for me. Just tell me what to do, and what I'm doing wrong.'

He does. And it works. I can do it myself. Eureka! After the first one, it is easy. And there was no shouting, no impatience, no implications of lack of intelligence.

So it *is* possible to learn things without being made to feel an idiot for not knowing how to do it in the first place. There are ways of negotiating. I like it. I could easily become enamoured of this kind of treatment. It is a blessing we all have the sense to know that, and to make sure I do not transfer my dependence to Len.

☆     ☆

The funeral parlour is next. Wooden panelling. Plastic flowers. Discreet coughs, and an outfit and moustache on the gentleman behind the desk straight out of Dickens. It's like stepping back a couple of centuries, or into a different world.

Would I like oak or elm, lined or unlined?

Frankly I wouldn't like either. What I would like is my husband, whole and well, safe in his school, or County Hall. Anywhere other than where he is at the moment.

Len picks up the unspoken message, and suggests something suitable.

Anything. What does it matter? This is not important. The important part is over. Peter has gone. Only the shell remains, to be disposed of decently, and as quickly as possible. Please.

My mind flips back to dad's funeral. The coffin at the front of the church. Stark. Unavoidable. Me thinking, 'My dad's in there.'

And a gentler voice reminding. 'That's not your dad.'

The image of the butterfly again. Release. Freedom. Wholeness.

The details are nearly complete. Mr Bumble is talking about times, itinerary. I do a mental run-through of the journey. At midday: a main road, and the local shopping centre to negotiate. We will never make it in the time he is suggesting.

I express my doubts. The undertaker is reassuring.

'We've never been late yet,' he says.

'You'd better not be,' I retort. 'My husband was a stickler

for being ready on time, and he'll never forgive us if he's late for his own funeral.'

☆    ☆

Back home, I go to get something out of the deep freeze. I haven't baked for weeks, but various friends have kept us well stocked, and the freezer shop has done a roaring trade. I open the lid, and the handle comes off in my hand.

Peter is making sure I don't forget him already.

What will the children remember of him? The image of the last few days? Heaven forbid.

I search out some photos. Peter, belting along the beach playing hockey. Peter with his face covered in flour. Margaret's photo of him smiling through the jungle. My own favourite of him preaching from a sand pulpit, with the text 'God is love' in the sand.

When my dad died we couldn't bear to look at the photograph album — still can't. This time we need the photographs, and we need them in a prominent position.

☆    ☆

Next day, the letters have gathered a new impetus. Only now they are addressed to me. I open them. See the words, half-register their meaning. Take them away, someone. It's lovely to know that people care, that they thought so highly of Peter, but . . .

Mum understands, I had to deal with hers about dad. Now I know why they are so painful. Each one is a visual reminder that it has all really happened. Another nail in that bloody coffin.

'Why?' I rail at God. 'What possible motive could you have for allowing one of your servants to die at forty-one?'

Many others are asking the same question, including Debra.

'Why?' she grieves. 'When he was so good to others?'

I shake my head. 'I don't know,' I have to admit. 'But he could have been a rotter, and lived a life that was empty and shallow. At least he packed more into forty years than the majority manage to pack into twice that amount.'

It is small consolation. The greatest one is that Peter himself came to terms with the situation, that over those last weeks his consistent message was, 'I am happy.'

Debra nods in agreement. It is true. He was.

I could add, 'And the last thing he would want would be for us to be sad.' That would also be true. But it would be expecting the impossible.

☆ ☆

Shirley takes me to social security. She sorts out a pile of explanatory leaflets. They are as clear as mud. Something to do with widows, and pensions, single parent families. They can't possibly be anything to do with us.

'Next please.'

We cross to the desk. There is perspex panelling between us and the clerk, presumably to prevent him getting biffed on the nose when the clients get violent.

'Yes.'

'My husband died.'

'Pardon?'

'My husband died.'

'Lord, do I really have to shout it? In front of all these people. No wonder they need the perspex.'

The clerk addresses himself to Shirley.

'She needs these forms. Get her to fill in that and that.'

He pushes the forms towards us.

I feel like screaming. 'I am here you know. I may be under stress, but I am not totally incapable.'

Shirley is equally indignant. She seizes the forms.

'Let's get out, quick,' she orders.

We make an abrupt exit.

And people have to suffer this, week after week after week.

☆ ☆

We order the flowers. I am still on auto-pilot, determined that nobody will touch me, come near me, see my hurt.

The florist nearly undermines the defences.

'Who are they for?' she asks. 'Somebody close?'

I hear myself explaining. There are tears in her eyes. She has four children of her own, and is obviously identifying with what it would mean to her.

Come on. Come on. Don't be kind, I can't cope with it. Tell me the details. Get down to practicalities. A posy for Jen. A sheaf for the big ones. A cross from granny and grandad and me. We have shared Pete in life, it is only fitting we should share this final tribute. There will only be a few more family flowers. We are asking others to put their tributes to more positive causes. Peter would have preferred it.

'What about cards?'

'Cards?'

'To go on the flowers.'

'What? Oh yes, I suppose so. If we must.'

'In deepest sympathy? Fondest memory?'

Here we go. The ache of loss to be expressed in inanities. Just give me anything. I'll sort out the least offensive when we get home.

On the way out of the shop, I pause. There are some strips of forget-me-nots.

'Look Jen,' I say. 'Forget-me-nots. Do you want to plant one in the garden for daddy?'

She does a jig on the pavement, a big grin across her face.

We buy four. One for each of the children.

I think the older ones may decline the offer, but they each plant one, and when the dog digs up one of the plants they nearly lynch it.

☆　　☆

I search through Peter's wallet for his driving licence, to return it to Swansea, as instructed by one of the interminable forms.

There are four crisp, new five-pound notes inside. I give one to each of the children. A treat from dad. Something special to choose for themselves.

Jenny decides on a drum kit.

I am obviously going to regret this, but it couldn't really be more appropriate. Now daddy is 'better', she too can sing unto the Lord, as loud and as often as she likes. And Peter will not need to wince.

☆        ☆

At bedtime, we pause in my room. The sky is a deep turquoise. A single star twinkles through the branches of the sycamore tree.

'Look Jen,' I say. 'A star. Behind daddy's tree.'

When she is safely tucked in bed I sneak back for another look. There are more stars now, but ours is still the brightest. It must be the evening star. A line of poetry hums in my head.

'Look at the stars! Look, look up at the skies.

O look at all the firefolk sitting in the air.'

I am back at college, walking along the January streets with the stars in their myriads overhead, and my hand in Peter's overcoat pocket because I have forgotten my gloves. He, poor lad, doesn't quite know what to make of the strange creature beside him, spouting Gerard Manley Hopkins. His mind moves round motor-bike engines, trade unions, theology, facts and formulae.

Well, we had fair warning. We both knew what we were doing when we committed ourselves to one another. It has been a good fight. Even if we did make a botch of the last year. I shall miss you, Pete.

'Oh, Lord. Who would have thought a star would set the fountains flowing?'

The star is there, three nights running, before the leaves of the sycamore camouflage it.

☆        ☆

As far as I know, Deb still has not cried. Margaret does not talk about her feelings. I wonder if they are experiencing the same agony of emotions as I am . . . the loss, the guilt, the anger, the self-reproach? All the things we did not understand, the words and gestures that hurt so much. So many must have been because of his illness, being unable to cope with the thousand-and-one demands he had taken on when his body was not functioning as normal and his emotions could not cope with all the implications of what was happening. They must not think he had given up loving them. I must talk with them. Share my hurt, my feelings of inadequacy and guilt. Help them to understand, not blame themselves.

I have a mental image of Deb, tucked under Peter's arm in the cobbled side-streets of York four years ago, when we went on a pilgrimage to retrace her roots.

'That's how I think of dad and you,' I explain. 'With one arm round you, protecting you.'

She cocks her head on one side, and grins.

'Really?' she says.

'Really,' I reply — with the mental after-tag, 'and how on earth are we going to manage without those all-sheltering wings?'

☆      ☆

Pete . . . how much I underestimated all that you were for us.

'You never remember the good things,' he rebuked one day.

There is a certain truth in that. It is healing now that so many are adding to our store of good memories, letting me talk out the pain of the past few months. Me? Talking? It is hard to shut me up. I wonder if I am boring people, dragging them down by taking them through my valley bottoms? If I am, they are being very patient. It is as if all the pent-up emotions of the last forty years are tumbling in a jumbled heap around my ankles. Tread gently, you who hear. Somehow, sometime, I have to pick them up, and put myself back together again. Please don't add to the bruises.

☆      ☆

I think of mum and Ann, how freely they talked of dad and John and Dawn, how because of that they still feel part of the family. They are not just a painful amputation, cut off, forgotten.

'Lord, thank you for teaching me that lesson, for all our sakes.'

☆      ☆

I feel as if everything has been slowed, suspended. I can't cope with movement or noise, the world going on about me. I don't want to know about everyday affairs, cooking, shopping, cleaning, conversation. I arrange flowers, fiddle with unimportant things, notice the trivial — butterflies on a continental quilt, a card, a brooch, a pair of pants. I remember Ann, after Dawn had died, doing a jigsaw at five in the morning. Remote. Removed.

I wouldn't have patience to do a puzzle. I just lose myself, dreaming. I stare through the window, trying to work out a pattern. Sometimes it seems to fall into place. For an hour or two. Maybe one day I will understand.

☆   ☆

Hassle about the funeral arrangements shakes me back to reality. Where? When? What? Who? Food for people, afterwards? 'Oh God, do I really have to think about it, try to work out how other people's minds will react?' All I want is that all those who loved Peter should be able to take part if they wish, and that the kids, and granny and grandad, and I, should not be subjected to too much public torment.

Don't they know it's bad enough trying to come to terms with what has happened, acknowledging that it has, even?

We could never get Peter in an aeroplane, so I don't really know what jet-lag is like. I wonder if it's like what I am feeling? As though some vital part of me is missing. It hasn't caught up with itself yet.

☆   ☆

The children are watching a film about President Kennedy. The tension between the family and his other commitments is too close for comfort. I retreat to my room.

Oh, Pete. You idiot. Why did you have to push yourself so hard, get involved in all those things that so often left only the remnants of your time and energy for us? Why did you have to leave us for good, now?

Why, God? Why?

The words 'Well done my good and faithful servant' reverberate round my brain.

There's no answer to that, is there. Only it hurts, God. Oh, how it hurts.

The letters are still flooding in. It is an effort to read them, an even greater effort to reply. I feel guilty about it when people have struggled to find the right words to express their love and concern. Maybe one day they will be less painful? Granny and grandad read and re-read them. I promise myself we will stick some of them in an album. They may be important to the children, later — especially little Jen. She will appreciate such gems as the one about Pete organizing the angels.

☆       ☆

Well . . . It has come. The day. The dreaded one. Switch on to overdrive. Stick there. That's one thing for which you can be grateful to grandmother — the ability to detach yourself, pull down the shutters, stop anyone seeing what is going on inside. If you can just keep going, cling to God. It will all be over in three hours, four.

People come, drink tea, stand around, hands in pockets, uncomfortable. Granny and grandad arrive. 'Lord, how do we help them?' I am beyond it. Locked in my impregnable fortress. If people think I don't care, so be it. That is the only way I know how to cope. Later, the tears will come. When I am alone. But I am sad for Peter's parents' sakes. Maybe they need to see me cry.

Maybe they don't. That they have been able to rally their own resources for this enormous ordeal is nothing short of miraculous. If I break down it could be the last straw.

Jenny comes to the rescue. Good old Jenny. Keep them talking, helping them cope, helping us all cope. Our mixed blessing. Sent for a purpose? So was that dog. Nobody can stay stiff and solemn for long with you two around.

☆       ☆

The children have chosen to come to the funeral. The two older ones know what it means. They came to grandad's. We had to explain the procedure to Deb and Jen. Deb is apprehensive. Jen thinks it is all one big celebration . . . lots of attention, auntie Shirley's bag of goodies to keep her quiet in the service, and a party afterwards. I wish I were only three.

Our extended family is swinging into action. Shirley,

Len, Janet, Chris, the curate. Poor Chris. He is taking the service. Little did he think that following in Peter's footsteps would come to such an abrupt end. Little did any of us.

Stop it, Wendy. Don't think. Talk. Do. Make another cup of tea. Answer the doorbell. Aunts, uncles, cousins. Family by marriage, family by adoption. Brothers and sisters in Christ. Their love is like a warm overcoat, wrapping us all inside. Only it is May, and I will not stay still long enough for anyone to hold me. I am restless, waiting, willing *them* to come. Fiddling with cups, tea towels, anything to keep my hands and mind occupied.

☆     ☆

A ripple of movement. They are here. Check coats, bags, hankies, the children, granny and grandad, that they each have someone to look after them. Half an hour and the worst part will be over. 'Help us, Lord. Hold us. Without you, I doubt I shall even make it over the doorstep.'

☆     ☆

We have negotiated the shopping centre, and the main road, and are crossing the stretch of grassland where cows graze loose. Jenny is chatting about model aeroplanes, parascending, circuses, all the activities she would normally associate with this area.

Not today, Jen. It's a working day. For those whose lives have not been so severely disrupted as ours.

We swing in through the gates of the cemetery. Trees, greenery, stillness, peace. Thank God. When we had the funeral service for dad, the church was on the edge of the town square. Everything was going on as usual. Cars, people, shops, bustle. It didn't seem right, somehow. When your world has come to such an abrupt standstill, it doesn't seem possible that life can continue as normal.

A moorhen jerks across a lily pond, as the car glides to a halt. That's OK. I can cope with that. But not the familiar faces, moving to open doors. Don't expect me to acknowledge you, or smile. It is taking all my energy to get out of the car, move forward, ignore what is going on nearby.

David is at my elbow. He looks so grown-up in a new leather jacket. Anxious. Protective. The girls look as apprehensive as I feel.

Come on, kids. Let's show 'em. You're a great bunch. Your dad would be proud of you.

☆   ☆

So many people. 'God, I can't go through with it.' I hate all this. Hate being on display. It's worse than getting married. That stretch of carpet to negotiate, seats at the front, everybody looking.

OK. Calm it. They're not here to watch, to look at you. They're here because they loved Peter. To support, not criticize. Get on with it. Now.

☆   ☆

The familiar words roll through my head. We stand, sit, sing, pray, give thanks for Peter. It has to be a service of thanksgiving, even if the words occasionally stick in the throats of those who are saying them. They're bound to. They too loved Peter.

It is nearly over. We are singing the hymn that expresses so many of the lessons we have learned over the last few months.

'O Joy, that seekest me through pain,
I cannot close my heart to thee . . .'

There is a swishing noise. I glance towards the coffin. It can't be the curtains moving. We haven't had the committal. I catch Chris's eye. He signals upwards. It is raining. We exchange grins as we sing the last few lines:

'I trace the rainbow through the rain,
And feel the promise is not vain,
That morn shall tearless be.'

☆   ☆

By the time we have come out of the crematorium, the sun is shining again. But raindrops still drip from the new

99

leaves, shaking overhead. We cannot see beyond the canopy of green, but surely, somewhere, just out of sight, there must be a rainbow.

PART TWO

# New Beginnings?

**T**HE DRAMA IS OVER. The principal character has gone. Those in the minor roles must find new outlets for their energies. I stay switched on to automatic; unable to acknowledge that, some day soon, I am going to have to start writing a new script for myself. My mother is left with the unenviable task of ensuring that the old set is dismantled.

She organizes me into clearing the garage, the wardrobe, Peter's study. Left to myself it would take a month of Sundays. The best things go to those who will make good use of them. The rubbish is offloaded on to the dustman, the rag and bone merchant, the council tip . . . anywhere we can dispose of it. Fast.

I collapse into bed at 1, 1.30 a.m. I will not, dare not, *think*. I keep expecting the garage door to grind open, and Pete to come in and tell us off because he won't be able to find anything, or to say that he needed the box of rusty nails we have just consigned to the bottom of the bin. There are sackloads of paper, boxes full of church accounts, school catalogues, mission publicity, bills dating back a decade. A tinful of letters from college days. I shove those to the back of the cabinet. Quickly. Maybe one day I will be able to bring myself to deal with them. Not now. There is solid ice where my heart should be. It is just as well. Otherwise mother and I would be standing in a permanent puddle.

&#9734;    &#9734;

A temporary thaw sets in with the discovery of last year's valentine card.

'Lucky me, having lucky you,' proclaim the words.

I hear Pete's voice, apologizing because he hasn't sent me one; me reassuring him that the previous year it was me who was distracted by other events.

I can see him furrowing his brow, asking 'Why?' Me reminding him that dad had died the day before. Him squeezing my hand.

I shake the memory from my mind. Oh, Pete. What have I lost? I can't think, daren't feel — yet. I still don't really believe it's all happened. What will I do when it does sink in?

☆     ☆

The children keep me going. Their lives have to go on. They have had a hard twelve months. They need to re-establish a routine, some semblance of normality. David has sport, and the imminence of his O-level exams to occupy his attention. Debra is playing steelband in the Town Show. Margaret is planning her summer wardrobe with her friend. They talk of pop stars, concerts, mini-dramas at school, the holidays. Ah. The holidays. I must do something about that.

'They want to go to Nefyn still, Lord.' Understandable, really. All their friends are there. I would go anywhere in the British Isles, the world, the universe, rather than Nefyn. Underneath, I know it would be a waste of effort. Wherever else I might try to take them they would only fret for the fun they could be having. Nefyn it will have to be. Or somewhere near enough for them to be involved, and far enough away for me to stay hidden until I can cope with it in my time, and on my terms.

☆     ☆

Jenny is a different proposition. At three years old you have not been indoctrinated into hiding your anxieties, camouflaging your hurt. Each day she presents me with a barrage of questions, comments, perceptions, which can leave me comforted in some small measure, or shell-shocked and disorientated. The rest of us may not be very good at communicating our feelings, but she more than makes up for it. While she is around, nobody is going to be allowed to forget Peter, or deny just how much his loss means.

☆     ☆

Unknown friends have sent gifts of money, for a treat. We choose a weekend of spoiling in a luxury hotel near Windsor. The children revel in the colour television in the bedroom, the chandeliers in the restaurant, the food, an outing to the safari park, my time and attention. Or the remnants of it. Part of me is still 'elsewhere', thinking 'How Peter would have loved it.'

His voice stops me in my tracks.

'What I have is far better,' it rebukes gently.

When I have recovered sufficiently, I share the experience with the children. They look pleased, but are non-committal.

A week later, Debra, Jenny and I are driving through Cranborne Chase on the edge of Dorset. The scene could have come straight out of a Hardy novel; gnarled trees, a tangle of hazels, bluebells carpeting the undergrowth.

'If heaven is better than this, it must be really something,' I sigh.

Deb nods. It might not be her ideal, but she's beginning to have a certain understanding of mine.

☆        ☆

'Lord, I reckon on average I lose three hours each day. It takes me so long to get started in the morning, and even longer to unwind at night. Dreams, memories, past, future, good, sad, roll through my mind in a never-ending procession. That last week. The last year. Peter in torment. Peter triumphant.

'Oh, God, I don't understand it. I only know that last night, those last weeks you were there; that no way were things out of your control. That other world was so real, so interwoven with this, it was not really 'other' at all. It was as if . . . as if . . . the barriers between are only of our making. If we have eyes to see, ears to listen, we will understand. We do . . . when the defences are down, and we are stripped of all that the world counts important.

'Now I am being absorbed back into the world. The walls are going up again, God. There are children to be fed, phones to be answered, work to do. It has to be so. We are spiritual beings, but we are bound by earthly bodies. I still have to live in the world, not retreat out of it. Only . . . I need these times of quiet, of putting together again, Lord. I cling to the comfort of Psalms. The heights, the depths, the agony, the ecstasy. It is all there. Others have walked through the valley of the shadow. I gain strength from their humanity, the fact that they do not deny their emotions, but hand them over into your keeping, for you to work upon.

'There's someone here who needs an awful lot of work upon them, Lord. Thank you that you seem to have a soft spot for the slow learners.'

☆　　☆

There are decisions to be made. The caravan is still sitting in the road from last summer. The roof is leaking. Peter was going to mend it. Do we sell it, or get it repaired, and try to find a permanent site for it?

Should I move out of the double bedroom and into the spare room, which is also my study, and far more sensible?

What about the car?

What *about* the car? I know it is a monster that gobbles petrol at an uneconomical and anti-ecological rate, but nobody is going to take that from me. It is part of Pete, and I am clinging on to it like grim death. Rust and all.

Strange how different things affect different people. Mum couldn't get theirs out of the drive quickly enough. I coerce David and the neighbour across the road into rubbing down the rust, and replacing a door that is about to drop off.

The rector's wife, whose two hobbies are rugby football and car maintenance, volunteers to service the engine. Her brother sorts out the caravan. Good. Now I have only to find a site for it. And make the transition to the spare bedroom.

I have a sneaking suspicion the site may be the easier to accomplish.

☆　　☆

I take a giant step forward and switch on the radio.

'Love lifts us up where we belong,' croons a voice.

I switch it off. Abruptly. It was the theme song of the last film we went to before Pete went into hospital. I can see him fidgeting in his seat, not really comfortable in any position, trying to smile reassuringly.

Oh, Pete. What an idiot I was. How little I understand. How many extra burdens I must have added to the ones you were already carrying. Can you ever forgive me? Can God? Maybe equally important . . . will I ever forgive myself?

I am back in the depths. Drowning.

'We're going to have to deal with this, God. Drastically. You know what a worrier I am. How I always believe the worst about myself. How I can't get through the general confession at the moment without leaking round the edges. It's all the 'if onlys'.

'I know all the rational arguments: Peter's choices, an unfortunate combination of circumstances, how others would have found the going just as tough. Friends do manage to talk some sense into me. But the accuser is always there, waiting his opportunity. You said this. You didn't do that. You killed your husband.

'Oh, God, what do we do about it? I know I made mistakes, many mistakes. Am I going to be bound by them for the rest of my life? Dragged down by the deceiver so that I can't work, don't sleep, can't care for the children as I should? The theology is familiar enough. There is sufficient in scripture to leave no doubt that you forgive all those who turn to you. Old Testament, Gospels, letters, all tell the same story:

'"I confessed my sins to you; I did not conceal my wrongdoings. I decided to confess them to you, and you forgave all my transgressions," says the psalmist. And that was written centuries before Jesus showed us just how much God loves us.

'So, why am I getting so wound up? Who do I believe? The Son, who offers forgiveness, love, acceptance, peace? Or Satan, whose handiwork is condemnation, fear, guilt, powerlessness?'

That's it. Spiritual warfare. The daily battle. A recurring one, knowing me and my personality. Get it down on paper, Wendy. A chart of the opposing forces. A constant visual reminder to be pinned on the back of the wardrobe door: who do you believe? Then every time you reach for a hairbrush or a hanky, it is there to remind you, along with some of God's promises of love and forgiveness. Right. That should nail him. Till the next time. I know I am going to need that wardrobe door. Frequently.

☆     ☆

Jenny is being her usual revolting self at the meal table. The food is too hot, or too cold. Or she doesn't like it. I try to be patient, to make allowances. It is late in the day for a three-year-old to eat. But it is the only time we are all together as a family. She is vying for attention with four much bigger people. She has to make her presence felt. She is succeeding! Usually, common sense prevails, but today, for some reason, I have had enough.

'Upstairs,' I roar.

She roars even louder when she sees I mean it. Her screams continue all the way up the stairs, along the landing, and into her room. I shut the door on them, so that the rest of us can continue our meal in semi-peace. Over the dessert I juggle mentally with the problem of how to balance compassion for a toddler who has lost a parent, with the obvious need for firmness and discipline.

Meal over, I sneak upstairs, coffee in hand. It is ominously silent. She can't possibly be asleep. She never gives in till nine or ten o'clock. She is not asleep. She is lying on the floor, wrapped in the sheepskin rug that Peter and the children brought back as a present from Wales the year she was born.

She points up to the wall, to a photograph of Peter holding her, when she was about nine months old.

'I like my daddy's photo,' she says. 'Every night before I go to bed I look at him. I sometimes talk to daddy through the glass.'

'So do I,' I sigh, putting down my coffee, and sinking on to her bed.

She scrambles onto my lap.

'I wonder if anyone else's daddy has died,' she says conversationally.

'Here we go, God. Today's bouquet of barbed wire.'

'Yes,' I reply. 'Martyn and Kelvin's daddy died, and my daddy — Grandad Williams.'

'Do you know any mummy who's died?'

Ah. I'm sure that I must, but mercifully cannot think of any immediately. Anyway, that's not what she's really after. Here it comes.

'Will *you* die?'

I know all the theological answers, and I am not using them. This little one needs reassurance on a practical level.

'Not if I can help it, and not until God's ready.'

Quick as a flash the arrow comes: 'Daddy wasn't ready.'

I nuzzle her hair, which will never quite lie flat and whisper, 'Oh yes, he was. At the end. He went gladly to God. He even told him to get a move on.'

She giggles. That figures. He would.

It might help if I could accept the logical explanations. Instead a string of 'if onlys' chase one another through my head. If only the doctor had sent him to the hospital sooner. If only I had realized it was not just psychosomatic. If only the doctors at the hospital had not let us go on clinging to false hopes.

If the scientists can reconstruct pictures of Mars, surely they can tell more accurately what's going on inside the human body, and without so many delays?

'I am angry, God. Very angry. With you, the doctors, Peter, but above all with myself, though I dare not always admit it!'

A cheque plops through the letter-box. Insurance money. One of the provisions we had made for the children should anything happen to either of us. Blood money. I want nothing to do with it. What value is money? I want Peter's arms around me, his chest to snuggle against, even his jacket dumped in the hall. I know I should be grateful that we will not have any financial worries. I am not. If it were not for the restraining influence of two well-trusted friends who are helping to sort out our finances I dread to think what I might do with it.

I am sitting on the bed, brushing my hair. Jenny plonks herself on my lap.

'Give me cuddles,' she instructs.

I squeeze her to me. The dog barks, and cocks her head on one side. She wants a fuss too.

'Ah. Nice little Jenny,' I tease, squeezing her harder.

The dog cannot contain herself. She jumps on to the bed, and starts nipping at the exposed bits of Jenny. She stops suddenly. She has caught sight of herself in the dressing-table mirror. She looks perplexed, then takes one almighty leap at the mirror and lands in the dressing-table drawer. Jenny and I collapse in peals of laughter. You should see the expression on her face. It is as much as to say, 'How on earth did I get here?'

'Oh, Lord, thank you for the gift of laughter. It is as healing as tears.'

Next day I am back in the depths, and furious with myself. I am not going to sink into self pity. OK, I am a woman alone. So are many others, and in far less favourable circumstances. We have a home, an adequate income, and dozens of friends I can sag on when the load becomes too heavy for one pair of shoulders. The paperwork is under control, car and house maintenance a minor irritation to be dealt with by those who know far more about it than I have any intention of ever discovering. The children have always been mainly my responsibility.

So, what have I to beef about? As if I didn't know. Peter is gone. As surely as that aeroplane disappearing into the distance. Yes. I know it's still there. It's just that I can't see it. That's the problem. I can't see Peter. Will never, ever in this life be able to reach out and touch him, tell him I love him. And there's no one to wrap me in his arms and tell me he loves me.

I need to feel good: to have clean clothes, my hair well cut, my room tidy. When things get bad I treat myself to a bunch of flowers, or drop hints to the children. Heavily. I order new wardrobes, bookshelves, a cane headboard, and make the transition to the spare bedroom. I buy two skirts and three blouses in the sales. Extravagance, or compensation? Trying to make up for what I have lost?

Mercifully I have read enough to know that there are certain emotions common to bereavement: shock, anger, relief, numbness, disbelief. I wrack my brain but can't remember anything about this. It makes sense, though.

I ask Shirley about it.

She says, matter-of-factly, 'It is human nature to try to replace.'

I must have a *very* human nature. Set any unattached male within dreaming distance, and my mind goes leaping, rushing, gambolling ahead. Possibilities of new beginnings? Come off it, Wendy. You haven't come to terms with the old ending yet.

I sigh. I seem to sigh a lot these days. Another symptom? It's a good job I've got the ability to laugh at myself. I need it. I may not see eye to eye with St Paul about his attitude to women, but most of what he says about young widows is spot on. Well, for this particular, not-so-young widow, anyway. Widow? How I hate that word. It is old, sober, grey. I do not feel old. I am not always sober, and I am trying to ignore the changing colour of my hair. Anyway, is it any wonder if there are a few more silver streaks?

'You know what happened today, don't you, God? I was looking for a passage of scripture in my old Bible, and it opened on the fly leaf. Wham. Straight between the eyes:

'"To Wendy. With all my love in the Lord Jesus. On your 21st. Peter."

'Remember what else he gave me? A set of frilly undies. We got that right, at least. Spirituality. Sexuality. They're both about letting go of yourself, aren't they? Responding to another? So where's the conflict?

'You are the ground of my spiritual being, God. You will always be. But I have shared my physical life with another human for eighteen years. I am an only child. There were only three months at the beginning of college when there was not someone there for me. You moulded me, God.

You were the one who said, 'It is not good for man to be alone.' Presumably the same holds true for woman.

'So. What are you going to do about it?'

☆     ☆

I open the Psalms. I have a feeling I am going to be stuck on them for several months. I read.

'Be calm before the Lord
and wait patiently for him to act.
Don't be worried.
It won't do you any good.'

'Don't be stupid like a horse or mule,
which must be controlled with a bit and bridle
to make it obey you.'

'I will teach you. I will instruct you and advise you.'

It is just as well. I need somebody to take me in hand. I add the verses to those already on my wardrobe door. I shall run out of space soon. I snort. Horse or mule indeed. That is not a very flattering image. And I certainly don't appreciate the bit about patience.

How come you invariably manage to home in on our weakest spots, God? And, I know I asked, but do you always have to have the last word?'

☆     ☆

It is June, and David has just finished his chemistry exam. Margaret is exhibiting her latest shade of nail varnish. It is good to see them relaxing. Margaret has not been 'with us' for several days. Teenage traumas? A chip off the old block? Either way it does not make for easy living. I hug her to me, and tell her it is good to have the happy Margaret back.

Half an hour later she is having a verbal punch up with Debra to celebrate. Jenny comes in bubbling with excitement. They are going to have a Caribbean carnival at nursery school, and she got two stars for a picture. Afraid of remaining unnoticed in the general hubbub, the dog chews through the telephone wires.

112

I trudge to the nearest unvandalized call-box, and phone the engineer.

'Er . . . My dog's chewed through the telephone wire. Can you see to it?'

He chuckles. 'The telephone? Or the dog?' he asks.

He sounds nice. I wonder if he's married?

☆      ☆

I am walking home from nursery with one of the other mums. Somehow we have got on to the subject of Peter. Must be Jenny. She was throwing another paddy when I left her.

'How do you cope?' she says. 'I don't know what my children would do if anything happened to their father. They're all daddy's girls.'

We part on the corner of the street. Our neighbour from across the road is just going off to work. She asks how we are. I spread my hands in a gesture of helplessness. She understands. Her family have had more than their fair share of personal tragedies.

'It makes me very bitter,' she explodes. 'How can there be a God?'

I hope the priests of her church are able to give a more articulate answer than I can muster.

Indoors the phone is ringing. It is a young man who was in the same ward as Peter. He wants to know how he is.

☆      ☆

It is evening, the same day. I snap Jenny out of the bath, and into bed. I am tired, dragging myself through the motions of everyday living. Perhaps a bath would help?

It wouldn't. A quick soak and I have had enough.

Too many late nights? It is rarely midnight before I switch off the light, but I don't think it is just that.

A touch of depression setting in? It would hardly be surprising. That's one stage I seem to have escaped so far. I seem to have swung to the other extreme. Hyperactivity, I think they call it. Come on. Calm down.

Into bed, Wendy. Lose yourself in a book. I pick one off

the shelf but it looks awful. A railway platform paperback. Two pages in, and I am hooked. It is about a woman coming to terms with a marriage break-up. All the emotions are there: desertion, rejection, guilt, failure, despair. The divorced ones are not kidding when they say 'Death must be easier.'

Poor Pete. I've always said I don't begrudge you to God, but I would have been devastated if you had gone off with another woman.

That's done it. The floodgates are opening. Oh, love. I miss you. I want you.

David comes in to ask something. He takes one look at me and changes the question.

'Do you want a drink?' he asks.

I sniff a reply, and he fetches me a glass of sherry.

'You know what they say about it being mother's ruin,' he teases.

'That's gin,' I retort. 'But it's no joke. It could be all too true.'

It's so easy . . . to reach for the bottle that deadens the pain. Temporarily.

'Trusting in the wrong spirit,' one of Pete's mates calls it.

'He's right, Lord, but it does help me relax, a little. And I have no intention of becoming dependent on it. If necessary it will stay on the supermarket shelf unless we have visitors. But tonight I need something to help me unwind. A little wine for my health's sake? It's been a tough day, God. Thank you that at the end of it I can share it with you and, despite the traumas, lie down in peace, and sleep.'

☆     ☆

Ray rings to check how we are. He has been working on the electrics in church, and missing his mate.

I chat to Len. He describes how the relief, the sense of rightness, is giving way to the realization that Peter has really gone.

The school secretary calls. She has a new electric typewriter, but can't bring herself to use it, because she keeps thinking about how Peter would have enjoyed experimenting with it. She talks about his illness. Explains how she knew he was not right for a year but thought it was the ulcers, and didn't get really concerned until after Christmas. Tells how he covered up, brushed off enquiries, said he wasn't worried.

The stories have a familiar ring. It is comforting to know I am not alone.

☆    ☆

Doreen's husband has died. I ache for her. The emptiness. Two other friends have heart attacks. Come on, you men. What are you doing to yourselves? There's Pete. Dad. And David Watson, who believed so strongly in God's power to heal, is still on the sick list. I thought it was the women who were supposed to be the weaker sex?

Ray calls in to see how long a list of odd jobs I am managing to accumulate for him. I think of his commitments to his own family, his job, the church.

'You're not overdoing it, are you?' I enquire anxiously.

He laughs. 'No. I know my limits. I learned the hard way.'

Alleluia. At least there is one sane male.

☆    ☆

I go to the requiem mass for Doreen's husband. Rod was another one, like Pete, who trusted in God and was not defeated. After the tears, we have lunch in Doreen's lovely garden. She is talking, pouring wine, making sure that people have everything they need. Only her eyes betray her. They are looking beyond the guests, the garden, searching some other country.

She tells a tale of Rod, lovable, laid-back Rod, coming in from the village where he has met the local undertaker. He has some surplus coffins. Could they keep one in the garage? It wouldn't get in the way. He could use it as a workbench.

Doreen protests. Rod argues, 'It's a lovely bit of wood, Dor.'

Eventually she explodes. 'I have learned to live with ten

115

televisions in pieces in the bedroom, but no way are we going to have a coffin in the garage.'

People laugh nervously. Unsure whether they should, or not.

Doreen, how do you do it? As if I didn't know. You do it because you have to, and if you didn't you would be lying in a darkened room stoned out of your mind on drugs. Not that part of your mind isn't dead anyway, refusing to function, unable to believe it has really happened. Someone at church called that numbness 'God's kindness', a safety valve, to help you cope when things get too painful.

It is only afterwards, when the anaesthetic begins to wear off, that each day becomes a series of 'ouches'. There are so many reminders. A man on a Honda in a red crash helmet, a letter addressed to P.K. Green, a blue checked shirt. You wind yourself up for the big things. It's the little ones that send you crashing.

Like the friend you haven't seen for a couple of years, asking, 'Hello. How are you?' You know what the next question will be before she opens her mouth. But it's too late. The defences are down. The shutters fly open. You are forced to acknowledge reality, put the unspeakable into words. Peter is dead.

'There's no way round it, is there God. You can avoid it, ignore it, rush around like a mad thing so there is no time to think. Sooner or later it catches up with you. Then thump. Down to the depths. Back howling it all out to you.

'Do you mind having a soggy shoulder most of the time? One blessing, at least I've never felt it was a personal vendetta on your part, some punishment for misbehaviour, or disbelief. I suppose the books have helped in that respect, the record of sorrows over many generations. It sets our own in perspective, somehow. Scripture too. Ecclesiastes:

"To everything there is a season, and a time to every purpose under heaven.
A time to be born, and a time to die;
A time to weep, and a time to laugh;
A time to mourn, and a time to dance.
A time to get, and a time to lose."

'That doesn't pull any punches, does it? Ah well. It helps to know there is a pattern. The good times, and the bad. That the weeping is part of the plan. There is no need to be ashamed.

'Help me to remember that, when I blank off, switch back into overdrive, push people away, pretend I'm all right. You know the reasons why. I can cope if you understand. Those words, so stark in their simplicity when his friend Lazarus died: "Jesus wept." How did you feel when Jesus was crucified? Did it seem as if the universe should stand still? Who did *you* argue it out with?

'You don't mind me arguing, do you? Telling you what I think? I'm afraid it could go on for some time. I doubt if I shall be able to come to terms with your purposes overnight. I'm too personally involved. The experts reckon it takes between two and five years to come to some form of acceptance. So far we've survived . . . what . . . two months? Seems like a lifetime. Still, death of a spouse does come top of the stress ratings. I suppose I've got to take it out on someone. And your shoulders must be broad enough, even if they are rather damp. Besides, answering back is a sign of security, so they say. Must be part of my new-found confidence in you. After all we've been through together, I *know* you won't reject, or abandon me.'

☆　　☆

It is nearly dark. I stand looking at my tree, branches silhouetted against the London sky. The chorus, 'Be still and know that I am God', hums in my head.

'Lord, thank you for stillness. For trees. For my tree. This reminder of all that Peter was for us. A strength, a shelter.'

I can hear the older children in the lounge. Life continuing, growing, developing. One of your sadnesses, Pete . . . that you wouldn't see them grow to maturity. I'm doing my best, darling, but you know I'm not the world's most dedicated mother, and there are so many things that could go wrong.

'Lord, watch over them, that their roots may go deep, and that they may be strong — in you.'

☆     ☆

I absorb myself in my work. I am on contract to finish a book by July. I didn't start writing it until June. The publishers are understanding. They give me an extension to Christmas. I am going to need it. The subject is, 'The future of the family.'

☆     ☆

Various people offer me part-time teaching jobs. They might be a good idea. Get me out of the house, occupy my mind. But I know I haven't the emotional energy to handle a class of children. It is taking all my stamina to get through each day, to keep things together for my own children. If I start giving too much to others, what will be left for them at the end of the day?

☆     ☆

I go to see David's teacher about his future options. David reckons he wants to be an architect. She says he could do anything he likes — if he puts his mind to it. When I return, Margaret is on the phone to one of the boys in her class. She is talking with a freedom we rarely hear at home, and looks so pretty in a summer top, pink shorts, and her hair pulled back into a pony tail.

They're growing up quickly, Pete. Inevitable, I suppose, after the last twelve months. Some days I feel as if I've aged ten years. It's left its mark on them, too. They are more mature. They see beyond the superficialities — sometimes.

It's not always as relaxed as this. Over tea, I had to bawl them out after yet another fight about the distribution of jobs. And I could have murdered Deb for calling Margaret a pig, when Len and Shirley were here — even if Shirley did reckon that was comparatively calm.

The trouble is, you expect so much of those closest to you. Like I did of you. I needed you to be interested in my world, my concerns, to talk about the things that should have been of importance to us. I didn't want to have to turn to others. It felt like a betrayal. Was I wrong? Was it too difficult for you to share the anxieties that must have been tormenting you those last twelve months? Were you even trying to protect us, in some strange way, as I was you — and probably made the situation ten times worse.

I don't know. We're such complex creatures.

'Only help me, Lord, to learn from my mistakes. Not to put too much on these children, especially David. So many people have already tried to label him "man of the house".'

'Help me to know how to resist this tendency. He has his own life to lead. He will be gone in two years, anyway. It is right he should go. No way must he think he has to carry the responsibility for me, or the girls, other than in the day-to-day practicalities which are part of an inter-dependent unit.

'Don't let me tie him, or the girls, to my apron strings to make up for the gap Peter has left. Only let me provide a secure base from which they have confidence to go out into the world. As you send us out; loved, equipped, liberated. In full knowledge that at the end of the day we can come scuttling back and your arms will be there to receive us, and hold us, till we are fit to face the hurly burly once again.'

☆    ☆

I listen to a man talking about how literature portrays, heightens, orders emotions. Four hours' later I am hunched in an office doorway, sobbing my heart out because a play has come too close for comfort.

I am so brittle still, so vulnerable. The slightest thing can set the fountains flowing. A book, a patch of lobelia, a talk on the radio, music. Music? Isn't that supposed to have power to soothe the savage breast? It just sets mine heaving. Choruses, hymns, a pop song, the classics. It makes little difference. Music strikes straight through to the inner core; exposes all the sufferings, hopes, dreams, we normally manage to keep hidden, even from ourselves.

Church has become an agony. There's hardly a hymn or chorus that doesn't launch some bolt from the blue. Even St Francis, bless him:

'O master, grant that I may never seek . . . so much to be consoled as to console.'

I can't sing it. It's not true for me at this moment. I need consolation, people to reassure me, hug me, listen to me, share their own sense of loss. Those who can cope with me scattering rainbows round the kitchen, and who don't retreat when I tell them it looks like being a long, wet summer.

☆    ☆

July has nearly come to an end. It is time to wind down my work in readiness for the holidays. I read the few chapters I have managed to write. To my amazement they are actually coherent.

☆    ☆

I seem to be fighting a losing battle with church. Praise? Worship? Jubilation? I haven't got the energy. I need stillness, serenity, the space to listen, be calmed by God. This time next week we will be in Nefyn . . . and Peter will not be with us. I stand the service for an hour, then beat a retreat to the park — again. The children are getting used to my sudden exits. They will collect Jen from the crèche.

I sit on a log, and let the soothing effect of the greenness sink into me. I long for some mystical experience, a voice, a vision. It is as if God is rebuking me, telling me I must not come to depend on special experiences sent in extreme circumstances. I should have enough knowledge, experience, assurance of his love, to help me cope with the daily hassles. He is right, of course.

Some boys are kicking a ball around the football pitch. A dog tries to join in the game. I smile, and dry my tears. It is life-affirming. It gives me strength to go back to our car, and wait outside the church for the children. Nefyn I can only leave to God. Like Peter's death, it is far too big to handle alone.

☆    ☆

It is the last day at home. There is a long list of things to do. Bank, library, car, dog, packing, cleaning, Jenny's presents. It is her birthday tomorrow: she will be four. Her first birthday without Peter.

I am not going to think about it. There is too much to do, mercifully. Doreen calls in at midday. We talk about Rod and Pete, the pain of the memories, loss, our inability to give, the need of time and space to lick our wounds.

'It's tough, Lord. There's no getting beyond it. Each day brings a new set of hurdles.' I open my Bible. The Psalm I turn to is headed 'A Song of Praise and Thanksgiving'. You just have to be joking!

'Praise God with shouts of joy . . .

Say to God, "How wonderful are the things you do!" (Letting Peter die? Wonderful?)

'Come and see what God has done,
his wonderful acts among men.
He changed the sea into dry land;
our ancestors crossed the river on foot.'

Yes, well. I suppose it was just as tough for them. Moving out into the unknown. Leaving the familiar. Finding new obstacles.

'We went through fire and flood.'
You can say that again.

'But now you have brought us to a place of safety.'
I suppose you have.

Peter is safe. We are surviving — just.

'God has indeed heard me;
he has listened to my prayer.'

All right, God, you win. I *will* try to praise you. Even though there are tears in my eyes.

☆          ☆

August, and we are on our way to Nefyn. I have buttressed myself with every device I can think of to make it more bearable. My mother and aunt are the first line of defence. They are coming with us. Once there, the older children can do their own thing. There are dozens of tiny bays around the peninsula. We can happily lose ourselves for a fortnight without setting foot in Nefyn, if necessary. I am almost happy as we drive through the hop-strung valley of the Teme, along the foothills where I was born, past Ludlow, into the edges of the Welsh border country.

Oh, this I had not foreseen. That holiday in May last year. The two of us . . . alone . . . in a field of buttercups; a hill fort, a post bus, a disconcerted minnow.

Conversations ebb and flow around my ears. I concentrate on the road. I dare not look at this countryside which I have always loved so much. Each mile is alive with memories. Compared to that, driving into Nefyn is a piece of cake.

I wonder how the children will cope, how they are handling the memories? Jenny has two doting adults to feed her ice-cream, lemonade and chips. She's doing all right. So are the two older ones, now the first twenty-four hours are over. It's Deb who looks lost, who is needing all the hugs and cuddles those who were closest to Peter are giving her. She goes into the house that is used by the mission team, and comes away disconsolate.

'Dad wasn't there,' she grieves.

I know, Deb. Why do you think I won't go near the place if I can help it, don't want to sit on Nefyn beach? I know his influence is still here, and will remain for a good few years. That's not enough. My big, strong, powerful, energetic Peter is not. This year I have a single sleeping-bag. The voice over the loudspeakers at the barn dance is Chris's. It shouldn't be. It should be his.

☆　　☆

I take my courage in both hands and go into Nefyn village. In the little supermarket I meet four people. They all want to know how things are. It is understandable. Nefyn must have brought reality home to many others with a nasty shock. It is true, then. Not just a misprint on a prayer letter? They want reassurance, need to know of Peter's victory, to allay the fear that lurks at the back of all our minds, the unspoken question: How will I cope when it is my turn?

☆　　☆

122

I read, talk, lie in the sun, sleep, try not to dream. We grow golden with the sunshine. Unheard of for our fair-skinned family.

One evening, as I drive down the track to the farm where we are staying, a thorn tree is silhouetted against the sunset. The sky is streaked pink, with mare's tails hinting a stormy day ahead. I stop the car. I ache for Pete, but the words of a hymn based on Psalm 8 are on my lips.

'When I think of thy heavens
The work of thy fingers,
The moon and the stars which thou hast ordained —
What is man in thy memory,
A man that thou mindest,
The son of man that thou carest for him?'

'It sets us in perspective, doesn't it, God? Eternity. Infinity. It is too much for feeble-minded mortals to comprehend. I know I am still asking "Why?", "What now?"

'Thank you that underneath is the certainty that you are, and that you are still in control.'

And, as if to reinforce that fact, above the dark heap that is Garn Fadron a single star is shining, bright against the velvet dark.

☆       ☆

Before we leave, we spend a day on Nefyn beach. Margaret throws a tantrum, Jenny nearly drowns herself, Deb stays close at my heels, and David does his usual 'let's-kid-the-older-generation-along' routine. It is not a restful experience, but it has laid another ghost. Next year when we come back, as I know the children will insist, there will be no 'first times' to face.

☆       ☆

We go to Greenbelt, a Christian pop music festival. The older children are in their element. Freedom, friends, fresh air, non-stop entertainment, rolling into bed at 2 a.m. I busy myself preparing meals, ferrying folk backwards and forwards to the station, listening to the seminars, trying to read by torchlight in the darkness of the tent when Jenny is sleeping. It works. On and off. But

I can't get beyond the basic ache. There are 27,000 people here, and I feel lonely. The one who would normally be beside me, voicing his approval or disapproval of the speakers, or simply sitting with his nose in a newspaper, is not here. If he were, I would not be reading by torchlight.

I keep Jenny up so I can go to the Cliff Richard concert. Just as he is about to come on stage she drops off to sleep. Never mind. She is wrapped in a blanket in her pushchair. I can listen in peace. But Cliff fails to weave his usual spell. I am restless, impatient, tired. I start to haul the pushchair across the lumpy grass. I don't know why. I won't be able to get to sleep if I go to bed. I am obviously getting too old for inflatable mattresses, noisy teenagers, and even noisier pop songs.

The mood of the music changes. It is dreamy, melancholy. Oh, Cliff. Did you have to include 'Miss you, nights'? At home I always push the 'fast forward' button on the tape recorder when we get to that one. I can't do that here. The words follow me across the field.

Oh, Pete. My love.

☆     ☆

I am reading Psalm 116, reluctantly. I can't concentrate. I am not in the mood. Maybe the heading has something to do with it? 'A man saved from death praises God.' Who wouldn't? And what about those who are not saved? Oh well, maybe it will throw some light on the subject? Come on. Let's get it over:

'The horrors of the grave closed in on me;
I was filled with fear and anxiety.'

I am back with Pete and that last year. How much of his stress must have been related to the terrible fears lurking at the back of his mind. What peace there was, those last few weeks, when it was faced and handed over to God.

'That helps, Lord, the knowledge that he died trusting you, that there was such a very real awareness of your presence. But where does it leave us? There is a big gap, Lord, where he should be. He was fun, for all his faults. He added so much to our lives.' Verse fifteen draws me back to the printed page.

'How painful it is to the Lord
when one of his people dies.'

'What's that? You mean it? You share that sense of loss?
Of something good gone from your world? Really?

'Can we write that in tablets of stone, for all who have
little appreciation of what it is like, who expect those who
have lost someone they love to be "snapping out of it",
when in actual fact it is only just beginning to sink in?'

☆      ☆

We get back to London. David's exam results have arrived.
He grabs the envelope and rushes up to his room. I wait
with baited breath. Peter died just three weeks before the
exams started. What effect will that have had? I think
maybe he will have scraped through the ones he was fairly
confident about, but will probably have to re-take a couple
in November. It will be understandable in the circumstances.

He emerges from his room waving a sheet of paper, a
grin from ear to ear.

He has six grade As, and three grade Bs, the best results
in the school. None of us can quite believe it. We leap
around the hall, rejoicing, hugging, so glad for him.

It is only later that the tears come. Peter would have
been so pleased for him.

☆      ☆

September. The autumn term has started. The children
are back in school. I can return to work, normality. Only it
is not normal. We have a young lad, Kevin, staying with us
temporarily, so at least there are six at the meal table once
again. But there is still something wrong. Someone is
missing.

We have been to Nefyn, but he wasn't there.

People tell me the school is empty without him, so he
can't be there.

He isn't in church, either. We are going to have to do
something about that. Each week I expect to see him
standing there in his white surplice, service book in hand,
outrageous sense of humour subdued for a while. It

knocks me for six each Sunday. Reopens the wounds, the sense of loss. I think I am going to have to concede defeat and worship elsewhere. At least then you might get a look in, God.

☆    ☆

The leaves are falling from my tree. The sky is grey. Summer is over. We have the long haul of autumn and winter ahead. All the firsts: Christmas, New Year, that terrible stretch before Easter . . . all the birthdays, Pete's, dad's, John's, Dawn's. All the memories. If we could go straight from Christmas to Whitsun and lose the months in between our whole family could be a lot happier.

'Lord, how am I going to cope?' How has Ann coped? Mum? I can feel my gullet clenching into a knot of tension, apprehension. My imagination is hurtling full pelt down the slope to disaster, as usual.

Stop it, Wendy. Look for the positive. So . . . it's September? That means you have coped . . . for what? May, June, July, August: four months. A third of a year. Only two-thirds to go. OK. So it's going to be tough. Nobody ever said it wouldn't be. But there's no way round it. You know that. You can evade, avoid, pretend it doesn't matter. It does. You shared your life with another for eighteen years. How can he go away, and you carry on as if nothing had happened? There are too many things to pin you down to reality. Like the words for that memorial stone you keep trying to forget about. It makes you wince? So it should. He was 'one of God's special people'. Go on. Have a good cry. At least it gets it out of your system. That's better than tying yourself up in psychosomatic knots, or sinking into self-pity: there's nothing to divert me, nobody has phoned, they no longer care.

What's the matter with your elbow? You're still capable of picking up a phone, aren't you? You've got an address book full of friends. What about reaching out to them for a change, instead of expecting their lives to revolve around yours? Invite them for a meal, a cup of coffee. Ask about their concerns, instead of always moaning on about yours.

He's not coming back. He isn't going to walk through

the door and sort out whether the house should be decorated, or provide some centre around which your life can revolve. You're on your own. So you'd better get used to it.

☆    ☆

I don't think I've ever known so many transitions of emotion as this, even in my teens. It might not be as bad if it didn't make me feel so ridiculously vulnerable. It's like living on a permanent emotional switchback. You haul yourself up the slope by your elbows or, rather, God hauls you by the scruff of the neck. And then the most trivial incident sends you zooming down the other side.

There are so many things that can throw you. Like the letter of probate.

'Be it known unto you that Peter Kenneth Green died . . .'

It's so harsh, so inescapable, and it's the one thing I'm trying not to know.

'It doesn't work, does it God? There are too many triggers. An autumn morning, golden leaves against a blue sky. Wham. I am back in the Wye Valley, two years ago, walking through the woods with Peter. Two days away from the pressures. The river is sparkling beneath us, some canoeists in red helmets are trying to negotiate the rapids. Peter is complaining that he is tired. I am laughing, and teasing him about teachers with no stamina. Was he ill then, Lord? He certainly couldn't eat or drink as much. And I just thought it was because he was getting older, smaller capacity.

'Smaller capacity. Ha! Oh, God, no wonder I don't want to remember. Couldn't the numbness last a couple of years, rather than a couple of months?'

☆    ☆

Jenny is presenting problems, though whether they are more to do with her behaviour or my reactions it is difficult to tell. She is so like Peter. The square shoulders, sultry lips, the same sharp intellect and incredible

127

memory. What's more to the point, the same determination. She just will not be told. You can reason, cajole, threaten. She always knows best — for herself, and everybody else. We try to tease her out of it, call her bossy boots, boss cat, but it doesn't make a lot of difference.

I try to disentangle how much of it is the result of the last few months, how much the 'frustrating four' phase, and how much the personality of this particular 'four'. It is impossible. Whatever the cause, one thing is certain — she can't be allowed to get away with it. She will be a very unhappy person in later life if she does.

'The best thing you can do for her is be firm,' says Len.

Right, Miss Jennifer. No more wheedling, manipulation, playing one off against the other. We will present a united front.

It is not as easy as it sounds. Invariably she manages to outflank us, or shoot the ground from under our feet with some seemingly simple statement.

Like *that* postcard. I am at my desk. She is playing contentedly with the things in her drawer. She pulls out a postcard. A couple of rhinoceroses at Windsor Safari park.

'Can you write this for me?' she asks.

The teacher in me obediently picks up a pen. She dictates.

'Jesus is my friend. I love him. Please can you help us, Jesus, now our daddy's died? Will you love us for ever and ever? Jenny.'

I write, but I don't know how. It is as if somebody has thrown a bucket of cold water straight in my face.

☆     ☆

The others appear to be coping. They don't say much, but I don't expect them to. Neither did I, when my grandmother died. I can remember dreading poeple coming towards me, knowing they were going to say something, and not knowing how to react. What do you say? 'It's OK.' But it's not. Religious jargon? No way. Tears? It's not the done thing. The best I could manage was a nervous grin, and a quick change of subject.

It's sad, but until someone teaches us to be less ashamed

of the emotions God has given us, it looks as though we're stuck with it. Ah well. I shall continue my policy of being open about how I feel, and sharing the things little Jenny says, in the hope they understand that I am trying to give them permission not to be ashamed of what is going on deep inside.

Saturdays reveal some of the depths. Peter, David and Margaret always used to go to see West Ham together. David is working in the local supermarket on Saturdays now, dismembering cauliflowers. Margaret wanders around like a lost waif. One week I fix for her to go to the match with another family, but she says it is not the same. She misses Peter's roars of approval, or disapproval; the running commentary on who shouldn't have done what, and why.

I'm sorry, Margaret. There's no way I can stand on the terraces for two hours, and the loudest response I could manage would be an anguished squeak if someone stepped on my toe.

David's biggest hurdle seems to be the Honda. He wants to use it, but there are practical problems to be surmounted, and I am worse than useless with anything mechanical. Various folk promise to advise him, and supervise his first tentative trips round the back streets. Somehow it always gets shelved.

I'm not sure if it's their busyness, my forgetfulness, or David's underlying reluctance actually to take over the machine.

A couple of days commuting to sixth-form college by bus solves the problem. The Honda is in the local motor-cycle shop being serviced, and David is teaching himself to ride, with a speed that takes us all by surprise.

☆     ☆

The three big ones are having one of their regular verbal skirmishes with our lodger.

'You just look what it says in the Bible,' he says.

Deb leaps to her feet.

'I don't know how you can believe in the Bible, or God,' she storms, 'when he killed my dad.'

Jen has switched to a different tack. She wants to know where I got Peter. Could I go back there? Who do I see when I go out in the evenings?

I know the way her mind is working. Mine gets stuck in a similar groove at regular intervals. I dread any male coming within five feet of her, in case she proposes on my behalf. *I* may need a course in assertiveness training. *She* certainly does not.

She drops another hint.

'We're lonely, aren't we, since daddy died?'

'We miss him,' I agree. 'But there's no need to feel lonely. We've got lots of people helping to look after us. Uncle Len, Ray, David . . . Isn't that enough?'

'No,' she says simply.

Exactly. Who was trying to kid whom?

The older ones are getting immune to my flights of fancy. They have seen it all before.

'It's not that I didn't love your dad,' I reassure them. 'It's just that he left such an enormous gap.'

They nod, understandingly. We talk about Peter's comment on that last evening, 'Let there be new beginnings', and whether that was his way of reminding me that we had always accepted that if anything happened to either of us the other should feel free to remarry.

Not that there is the remotest possibility. With four kids, and me on the wrong side of forty, the statistics are weighted pretty heavily against it. Besides, I know enough about marriages on the rebound, and my own psychological state, to tread very warily on that territory.

Not that that acts as a brake to my over-active imagination. It is still fizzing and popping in all directions.

'You should go out more,' David advises. 'Meet more people.'

'Find another man?' I retort wryly. 'I'd like to see your faces if I did.'

Jenny is obviously not satisfied with the response to her postcard. She wants a bit more action.

'We should ask Father Christmas,' she suggests. 'He might send us another daddy.'

☆        ☆

Debra manages to create a diversion by getting excluded from school. She is in the wrong. She knows it. But like the rest of humanity she finds it impossibly hard to admit. When confronted with her misdeeds she shrugs, sulks, pouts her bottom lip. It does not go down well with the teachers, understandably. It has never been particularly popular with her parents, either. She has to realize that there are limits, and reasons for those limits. If you violate them you must pay the penalty. A school with several hundred pupils cannot function as if there was only one person to consider.

On the other hand, the staff need to appreciate what must be going on inside Debra. Not only is she having to cope with the normal teenage identity crisis, she is fighting on at least three other fronts at the same time. A black child in a white family, who has already lost two parents by adoption, and is now having to handle the death of a third.

She is resentful, rebellious. Who wouldn't be? So am I. 'Please, God, help us to channel her anger into constructive channels. She has so much sparkle, vitality. It would be a tragedy to see it destroyed, or distorted.'

☆      ☆

We reach an unexpected oasis: granny's birthday. I have been dreading it for weeks, worrying how she would feel. On the actual day she is surrounded by people, presents, cards, flowers, love.

'This is the best birthday I've ever had,' she announces.

Strange, isn't it? Debra made a very similar remark about this year's holiday.

☆      ☆

I am reading Jenny a story about a grandad. He is seventy. An opportunity for a bit of conditioning?

'Your grandad is eighty,' I say. 'Ten years older than him. Aren't we lucky to have had him for so long?'

She looks at me doubtfully. She knows what I'm getting at. Another one of the family heading for heaven at some point in the future. I wonder what image she has of the God who has taken two of the four males who are important in her life, and who will one day deprive her of a third.

'Is heaven like a hospital?' she asks, answering part of my unspoken question. I swallow hard. 'Do you hear, God? Do you see what I mean?' I fumble for images a four-year-old will understand.

'No,' I reply. 'It's more like a party. Think of the excitement when you see Jesus, and how pleased grandad would be to be with daddy again.'

She appears to digest it, but regurgitates it three minutes later, with 'I don't want to go to be with daddy yet.'

'That's OK,' I reassure her. 'You're only four. People don't usually die till they're very old.'

She appears satisfied, but my brain is doing a quick calculation. Ann's Dawn was six, John in his early thirties, Peter forty-one, and my dad sixty-three.

So, I growl at the Almighty, why does it have to be our family that disproves the general rule?

☆   ☆

A speck of sunshine glimmers on the horizon; an invitation to a poetry reading. I know it is not everyone's ideal of an evening out but to me it spells relaxation, socializing, an opportunity to be stretched. The only problem is, it clashes with a previous commitment. If I cancel that, it could offend people, put me even lower in their estimation.

So be it. Those whose opinions I care about will understand. For the others, it will have to be one more step in their growth towards maturity. And mine.

'You must have taught me something, God. A few months ago I couldn't have reasoned like that. I would have been bound by others' expectations and demands; by duty rather than my needs. It feels terribly selfish, goes against all my previous programming, but that is where I'm at. I still need to have strength poured into me; I'm likely to for some time to come. You understand, don't you, God? So does Shirley. She's just told me off in no uncertain terms for agreeing to lead a meeting when I should still be in a receiving position. I don't know which is worse, acknowledging there are limits to how much I can give, or learning how to receive. It's all to do with pride, I suppose. The great self-sufficient 'I', having to admit dependence on others.

'That's yet another lesson you have had to teach me, as you have taken me apart, these last eighteen months. It hasn't been comfortable, God. I haven't liked what I have seen. But at least I now know what I am, and some of the reasons why. Help me to use this knowledge, not as an excuse, but as a weapon; to know right to my very core, that you do not give up on me. Thank you that although all my inner 'nasties' no longer lie hidden, you are saying, 'Right. I can live with them. Now . . . how about you?'

My prayer list gets longer by the day: people coping with illness, bereavement, broken relationships, the other loners.

'I joke about being surrounded by the walking wounded, but it's not funny, God. There are so many hurt and bewildered people in our society. Help me to know how, in some small way, I can share their pain. Others have been so good at taking mine.

'Strange, isn't it? It took just a few months to teach me how to talk, but it's taken thirty-odd years to rediscover how valuable that gift is. Teach me now to listen when others try to articulate their fears, or work out some shape and structure to their problems. I know now that there are no easy answers. I doubt that they would want to hear them if there were. Love is in the listening, taking the anger and the pain. And in the practical help: putting air in the car tyres, sorting out social security, and screwing the handle on the freezer.

Chris, the nurse, phones.

'How are you?' she asks. I tell her the truth. She can handle it.

'Is it the lack of adult companionship that's causing the problems?' she asks.

Got it in one, Chris.

'Do you want to come for a meal?'

Oh, Chris. Yes, please.

☆     ☆

The difficulty is getting the balance between my needs and those of the children. It is so easy to tip off the tightrope in either direction. I try not to go out more than a couple of times a week, to invite folk here whenever possible, but I still get complaints.

'Do you have to go out again?' Debra sulks, as I chivvy everyone through their evening meal. I look at her in surprise. I am used to having to prise Jenny from me like a limpet if she gets so much as a hint that I am about to set foot over the doorstep without her. Debra is a different proposition.

'Is she really upset if I go out?' I ask later.

'She doesn't seem to mind,' Margaret replies. 'Besides, you've got to go and meet people sometime, when you've been stuck here all day.'

Hooray. At least one has got the message. Why hasn't Debra? Am I overdoing it? Should I go easy for a while? But if I stay in, invariably I'm in my own room, reading, writing, on the phone. Is that it? Not just the going out, but lack of sufficient attention, showing up that empty gap where Peter should be?

'I miss daddy growling at us,' she admits one day.

'Miss being told off?' I query.

'No,' she says. 'I mean when he came in from school . . . how he used to hug us to him, and go "Grrr".'

Oh, Deb. It's so easy to see Jenny's need of cuddles, my own, even the dog's. A teenager cannot always afford to state hers so obviously. I must make a more conscious effort, be more interested in your life, your concerns. See your need of time and touch. Reassurance.

Half term presents an ideal opportunity. The older ones have friends to stay. They have organized their own programme. Jen, Deb and I take ourselves to St Albans.

We wander round the market, explore the back streets and bookshops, have lunch in a Berni Inn. The girls eye the desserts enviously. It is a luxury I had not contemplated, but a bit of spoiling may be just what they need.

'Can we afford them?' Deb asks, anxiously, when I ask if they would like one.

I think of my resentment, my reluctance to accept the fact that we probably now have more financial resources than ever before — and the reasons behind that reluctance. It is time for a change of gear.

'Yes,' I reply. 'You can thank your dad that you can enjoy the extras like this, because he made sure there would be sufficient for us.'

Well done, Wendy. Now you make sure it is not words only, that you begin to use that provision for the children, so that they still feel Peter is part of their lives in a very positive way.

Deb's eyes gleam with satisfaction as she tucks into her dessert. I should have spelt it out sooner. It is not the first time she has expressed concern about whether we might have to move house, or alter our lifestyle. Thank you, Peter, that neither have been necessary; that the children have not had that security eroded.

After lunch, we wander round the cathedral. By the shrine of St Alban candles gleam. The children pause, held by the warmth of light.

'Do you want to light one, and say a prayer of thanks for daddy?' I ask hesitantly. Jenny dances a jig. Debra nods.

They light them wonderingly, and kneel without being told. I expect the words to choke in my throat, but they stumble out somehow. It is a uniting and healing experience, a fitting memorial of all the light that Peter brought into our lives.

☆        ☆

A week later it is 5 November and we are celebrating bonfire night. None of us feels up to the joint festivities at church, or in the local park. There is a mound of garden rubbish to be burned, and Jenny can have a few sparklers. That will be sufficient. At least, that's the theory.

In practice we somehow manage to accumulate two boxes of fireworks, several packets of sparklers, a guy, an oven full of sausages and potatoes, a tray of cinder toffee, a saucepan full of popcorn, and several friends.

I fret about the teenagers being responsible for the fireworks, but they are in their element. It's the first bonfire night we have had at home for donkey's years. Praise be. No painful associations. I can relax, and enjoy the children's happiness.

☆      ☆

David is rolling round the lounge, laughing at some comedy programme on television.

'It sounds as if your dad would have enjoyed that,' I call to him.

'That's just what I was thinking,' comes the reply.

☆      ☆

The council erect new road signs outside the school next door.

'SLOW. 30 mph,' they proclaim.

The children can hardly get through the door fast enough.

'Seen the signs?' they scream. 'They must have seen you going down the road. What is it? Forty before you're in third gear?'

I've heard that kind of comment somewhere before, too, and from someone who would have been doing twice my speed.

☆      ☆

I take the children's books into the building society to have the half-yearly interest added. A sudden thought strikes me. The books are still in our joint names. I explain the situation to the girl behind the desk.

'That's easy, madam,' she assures me. 'Just bring in the death certificate. We can soon delete your husband's name.'

It is not 'easy', miss. It is one of the hardest things I have ever had to do.

☆    ☆

'I am on the run, God, filling the calendar with activities, rarely in bed before 1, 1.30 a.m., trying to halt the 3D, morning-noon-and-night presentation that is constantly projecting itself through my mind. The past is a turmoil of images triggered by the slightest association. The future holds Christmas, New Year, that dreadful block through January to Whitsun. The present I don't keep still long enough to find out about.

'A family anecdote flits through on cinema one. It shows a pre-school me running down a country lane, calling to an aunt, "Did you see Wendy Williams run past herself?"

'I'm still doing it, God. And falling flat on my nose in consequence. Whatever would I do if you weren't there to pick me up, dust me off, and start me all over again?'

☆    ☆

Christmas is coming. The turkey is in the freezer. And that's about all. Three weeks. Two. Stop the clock, someone. The world. Anything. Just don't let it happen.

The children want a tree. A real one. We have two plastic ones, a silver tinsel one, and a baby fir up the garden. They must have the real thing, even though we'll be away over the actual holiday. Oh well, I suppose it is small compensation. OK, kids, you have won your tree, provided you decorate it.

Chris, bless her, has made the Christmas cake. Left to me, I doubt if we would have had one.

Presents are a nightmare. They mean hauling myself back to reality, applying my mind to the everyday world.

Cards start to plop through the letter-box, a dozen at a time. All those people who supported us with so much love and prayer. They deserve to know how their prayers have been answered, how God is holding us, if I would only pause and recognize it. If someone would switch off the music it might be easier. Whoever would have thought that a carol service would dredge up so many memories, despite the fact that we have moved churches?

Halfway through 'Once in royal David's city' I nudge

Margaret. I point to the lines 'Tears and smiles like us he knew.'

'Just as well, isn't it?' I mumble. She grins. She's caught me often enough with a soggy hanky to know exactly what I'm talking about.

☆     ☆

Jenny has similar blockages. She will sing the first two verses of 'Away in a manger' with great gusto. No way can you get her to join in the third. She obviously is not ready to be 'fitted for heaven', and she has no intention of tempting Providence.

☆     ☆

I am trapped in a coach, heading north across the Cotswolds, to mother's. We are accompanied by the non-stop nostalgia of the pre-Christmas pop programmes. For the first time I begin to appreciate why the number of suicides rises with the season of tinsel and artificial goodwill. If only there weren't so many tear jerkers. It's David Essex at the moment, singing one of last year's hits.

'It was only a winter's tale,
Just another winter's tale
And why should the world take notice
Of one more love that's failed.'

Oh, Peter. Did we fail? Did you know how much we loved you? It was such tough going, that last year. I had to be the wicked witch so often . . . holding, restraining, trying to burrow through so many layers of defences. Did you know it was because I loved you, even when I didn't understand? Was that *why* I didn't understand? I just couldn't accept all those barriers between us?

'Lord, we're such idiots. We're so bad at conveying our feelings; telling others how much they mean to us. Especially those closest to us. Look at Shirley and Len. She has to face an operation now, and the only way they can cope is by joking about it. Two trained counsellors. What hope is there for the rest of us?

'Is that why your Son had to be crucified? Because we wouldn't believe mere words? We had to have a visual reminder, a constant image, which we couldn't forget? Some way of hammering into our dumb brains: God loves you, and walks beside you, sharing the darkness of your night.'

☆　　☆

Once we actually get to Christmas it is almost bearable. It was a good decision to get away. If we had been at home I know I would have been haunted by the memory of Peter, curled in the armchair in the corner of the lounge. This way there are fewer reminders, mother is spoiling me rotten, and the turkey can stay in the deep freeze till kingdom come.

Only one guilt nags at my mind: granny and grandad, stuck by themselves in Dorset. How are they coping, after so many Christmases with the grandchildren? What are they doing to pass the long hours, erase the memories? Arguing about what they should watch on the television?

We phone to check how they are. They are not at home. There is only one possibility. Someone from the local church has invited them to their home for Christmas dinner. Indeed they have and, what's more, they have accepted. I can hardly believe my ears. The age of miracles is not past. It is happening on the other end of the telephone.

☆　　☆

It is New Year's Eve, prelude to 1984. We are down in Dorset, staying with one of the families who do so much for granny and grandad. Jenny is tucked in the bed beside me. The family have gone down to the seafront to see a group of spartan swimmers go in for a midnight dip. The house is silent.

By any reckoning of my pessimistic character I should be feeling sorry for myself, dreading the New Year. But I am not. Looking back over 1983, I can only praise God for his help and strength, the miracles he worked in and for Peter. I am looking forward with an expectation of more miracles.

I would never have believed it possible. Is this fool-hardiness? Or part of that new-found confidence in the God we can 'rely on'?

I have even managed to wean myself off the Psalms. St Matthew's Gospel seemed more seasonal. Tonight's passage is an appropriate one for the New Year, especially one vested with so many gloomy prognoses. It tells of the call of the first disciples: Jesus beckoning, 'Come with me.' The words seem to convey a much closer relationship than the more usual 'Follow me.'

It is as if his hand is stretched towards me, drawing me on. I have only to stretch out my own hand and place it in his, and he will take me forward into whatever the future holds.

As rockets splutter over the seafront, heralding the New Year, I place it in God's hands, and lie down to sleep, content. And that, surely, is the first miracle of 1984.

☆　　☆

With the new year come new perceptions. I am less angry towards the doctors. The symptoms were so similar to ulcers. Peter was in a stress profession. Even I didn't panic until the New Year. Would earlier diagnosis have allevi-ated, or added to the hell of those last twelve months? David Watson and his family have had the awful shadow hanging over them all year. Was it God's mercy that we did not know until the last few weeks?

If it had been spelt out to us, would we have believed it? Wouldn't we still have indulged in the psychological gymnastics that prevent you acknowledging that your worst fears may actually be true?

As it was, Pete was still going into work until the day before he went into hospital. It only really sank in that he was not going to 'get better' the week before he died. Was it just coincidence that his condition deteriorated the day after he eventually acknowledged that fact? I don't know. I don't envy the doctors in the decisions they have to make. All I do know is that I shall find it very hard to believe anything a member of the medical profession ever says to me again.

☆　　☆

Someone is trying to disentangle a few of the knots in which I am currently wrapping myself.

'Did you have a good marriage?' he asks.

I laugh. Did we? It didn't feel like it at times, especially over those last turbulent twelve months.

Shirley tends to classify only children as disadvantaged. I am inclined to agree with her. We are not good in the rough and tumble of relationships. We are not used to handling conflict, competing for attention. It has always been ours by right. We like to be centre stage, receiving approval, acclaim, some response for our efforts. We don't know how to handle criticism, or rejection. We need people to need us, as Peter showed, in his over-involvement in so many causes.

Ah well. I didn't know *why* he was, when I married him, but I did know *what* he was. I went in with my eyes wide open. Nobody compelled me to the altar. Or him. We learned to live with one another over eighteen years.

When you know you are imperfect, it helps you make allowances for the imperfections in others — eventually. We made good sparring partners. The ache has been not because I was dependent on him, but because we were interdependent. As long as we needed one another, it was fine. The problems came when he was drawn into that lonely journey where none of us could accompany him, only distract his attention for a few hours along the way.

I sigh. So much falls into perspective with hindsight, which was pure hell at the time. If only he had articulated his fears. If only I had heard, understood.

I think of his secretary, commenting one day that he was so proud of me, and of the children. My eyebrows arched in surprise. Was he? Then why didn't he tell us? I can see now that he did, in the way he knew best, the practical things — making desks for the girls, setting up my study, sharing his love of sport with those who knew how to appreciate it. But we needed words as well. Or at least I did. And trying to condense his feelings into language was the one thing he found difficult. And I lacked the necessary skills to help him. Shirley reached through. She says he cried for an hour, an hour and a half, one day in hospital, grieving for what he would lose; the pain of not seeing the children grow up.

Ah well. At least we had those last few weeks; that precious time when we knew where we stood. No more denials, evasions, abortive attempts to protect one another from the harsh realities, which in some strange way were easier to handle than all the fears and misinterpretations of the previous year. Once we knew what we were dealing with, we were no longer walking alone. Even the silences conveyed a different meaning. And that last night. That special consciousness of God's love, his presence. Healing. Giving us the words, however inadequate.

Oh, Pete. Did we have a good marriage? Yes, my love. The tragedy is, we didn't appreciate just how good it was until it was too late.

'There's always some unfinished business in every relationship,' says Len. Is that one of the reasons why it's so much harder to come to terms with a sudden death? There's no opportunity to put things right?

'Lord, we pass one another so many negative messages, get so easily distracted from the things that are of real importance. Help us to learn how to tell our parents, partners, children, friends just how much we love them . . . while we have the time.'

☆    ☆

A friend is sitting in my car. We are talking about how Peter's death felt more like healing than defeat.

'For you, too,' she says. 'You seem changed, healed.'

'It made me more positive,' I muse aloud, 'more sure of God. Gave me a greater concern about relationships, an urgency to get them right,' I smile ruefully. 'I suppose I learned the hard way the value of what I have lost.'

She squeezes my hand. 'I'll pray you someone blue-eyed, rich and handsome,' she teases.

'You can forget that,' I retort. 'I have only two criteria. Somebody who would care about us, and is able to communicate his own needs. At least then there is some ground for negotiation; a possibility of bridging the inevitable rifts.'

I think about the conversation later. I don't need much of an excuse for that kind of daydreaming. Anything to carry me through the long, dark hours of winter, obliterate the loss. As long as I recognize that that is all it is. I know enough about relationships on the rebound, the temptation to compensate, the hunger for physical affection, to know that is not a firm enough basis for a permanent commitment. There are too many pressures on relationships in the modern world for them to be built on anything other than solid rock.

There is much more healing that still needs to happen in me. These last two years have dredged up so many fears and insecurities. My logic, my emotions and my Lord would need to tell the same story before I would have confidence to launch out into uncharted territories. Besides, although I will eat anything, when it comes to clothes, books, jewellery and men, I am very choosy. I would rather go without than make a wrong decision.

Are you listening, Wendy? Taking it in, ready for the next time you start fouling up valuable friendships with an over-enthusiastic response to perfectly normal expressions of affection? Stop living in cloud cuckoo land and concentrate on your fledglings for a change. They need love and affection just as much as you, you know.

Look at them with the dog, rough-housing her around the lounge. You worry about her breaking a leg but she always comes back for more. She makes a very good punch ball, as you know full well. You're not above taking your feelings out on her yourself. And who could sink into self-pity for long with her around. A couple of sniffles, and she is by your side, nuzzling your hand, dropping a slimy ball in your lap, looking at you with her big brown eyes as if to say, 'Don't cry. I'm here.'

Is that why Deb pleads to take her to bed every so often? It's not the dog that's lonely, but Deb? And you, lousy mum, only respond by telling her, if she is that concerned about the dog's welfare, maybe she could go and sleep in the kitchen.

You were wrong, Shirley. I wasn't suffering a brainstorm having that dog. She was the best thing that could have happened. Her love is so uncomplicated, and generously distributed among us all.

☆      ☆

'How's it going?' asks an acquaintance. I shrug the question away. Now is not the right time, or the right place, for the detailed answer an honest reply would involve. He misinterprets my reticence.

'Don't be too brave,' he warns.

Brave? That's the last word I would have used to describe myself. Remote, detached maybe — but there are reasons for that. It's something that I, as a teacher, should have recognized long ago, but it has taken a book on families to unearth it. The writer was describing an infant's response to separation from its mother as three stages: distress, despair, detachment.

I hear my mother telling the familiar tale of how they evacuated to Shropshire from the blitz, only to have me taken into hospital in Birmingham for treatment for eczema when I was six months old. When she was allowed to collect me three months later I didn't know her, and screamed to stay with the nurses.

So, it wasn't all my grandmother's fault, and no, I am not brave. I still switch to that third stage as soon as I think anyone, or anything, is likely to hurt me. I can feel myself switching to it now. Pete's birthday looms large on the horizon, then dad's and the anniversary of dad's death. I am not going to think about them. Up go the defences. I barricade my mind with all kinds of projects: alterations to the house, an evening out, plans, preparations, provisions. The unexpected still manages to undermine the best-laid strategies.

David is out on the Honda, and late; a friend has promised to phone, and hasn't; parting from someone special — things like these reopen the wounds, dig much deeper, to the loss I am trying to ignore, and can't, however furiously I fight.

☆      ☆

As I might have expected, coping with the reality of Peter's birthday is much easier than coping with my imaginary version of it. I have tried to fix for the three older ones to share a night out at the cinema, but David and Margaret have other plans. Jenny is blissfully ignorant of the implications of the date. That is one burden she need not bear. That leaves Deb and me. What can we possibly go to see? Our tastes are so diverse? There isn't a lot of choice. It boils down to one film.

'I don't know if you'll like it,' David warns.

From the review in the paper I doubt very much that I will. I am delightfully surprised. Five minutes into the supporting film and I am aching with laughter. It is set in a school and true to so many of the staff and pupils I have known. Deb is more amused by my reaction than she is by the film. It is a good evening. And I think, Peter, you would thoroughly approve.

☆      ☆

We have a bad week at half term. Too much spare time. Too many memories. I return home to find the knob on the cooker won't budge, the dog has made a mess on the kitchen floor, David broke his glasses at a pop concert, there's a letter with four photos of Peter — and the news that David Watson has died. My first instinct is to reach for the sherry bottle. Warning lights flash. With a super-human effort I manage to convince myself that the Bible study is cheaper and far less disastrous for the liver — and for the soul.

☆      ☆

By Friday I am coiled tight as a spring. I need to get to the West End shops and decide that walking will be a good release for the build-up of tense nervous energy. It relieves some of the physical symptoms, but cannot erase the memories that come crowding in from every quarter. I stand waiting for the traffic on an island in the middle of the road. I am exhausted, and the sense of lostness and aloneness has built to such a pitch I can empathize with those who decide to take the quick way out.

Fortunately I am too much of a coward to put the thought into action, but some form of diversion is obviously necessary. Maybe a cup of coffee and a slice of chocolate gateau will help? They do. So does the company of other people milling around the cafe. Blood sugar level and equanimity restored somewhat, I head towards the nearest bookshop.

I am browsing through the poetry section when I suddenly become aware that premenstrual tension could be contributing to the current nose-dive in my emotions. Now . . . what excuse can I find for the other three weeks of the month?

☆    ☆

1 March. Daffodils. Leeks. St David's Day. Wales. Dad. Oh! I'm only just getting over the other anniversaries — not that as well. More melancholia? Banish the thought. Turn it into thanksgiving: for all that I am, for all I have learned from him of gentleness, uprightness, respect for others. It doesn't deaden the ache, but you feel less distant, dad. Tell me, will I one day be able to turn the memories of Peter into praise, rather than wincing away from the pain?

☆    ☆

I continue my ongoing argument with God, but on a different tack. I seem to have changed from the 'If only's' to the 'Yes, buts'. Kevin senses the change and buys me a poster, a small animal with its paws clasped, nose turned heavenwards, and the words 'Yes, but . . . every time I try to see things your way I get a headache.' I don't, actually. I get an ache in the jaw, or a lump in the gullet. I try tranquillizers, sherry. Neither will shift it.

I know what I have to do; work through to some kind of acceptance. That will be the day! Accept that Peter has gone, that I may have to spend the rest of my life alone?

'Why not concentrate on something simple, like solving the Irish problem or the Arab–Israeli conflict, God? You'll get nowhere here.'

I phone Shirley to complain about my irritation with

myself, and the fact that I'm back on those wretched tablets. She appears to take it all as a matter of course.

'I don't know what you're worrying about,' she says. 'What do you expect? The only wonder is you've not ended up on them before.'

☆     ☆

I wake, shaking, from a dream. Jenny and I have been crossing a very rickety wooden bridge, erected high above a wide river. Lots of the planks and supports are missing, and both of us are petrified. She clings to me for safety, and I am very conscious of being solely responsible for getting her to the other side. As we begin to descend the steps on the farther side and I relax a little I suddenly realize she is no longer holding my hand. There is only one way she can possibly have gone. I rush down the steps and into the water, which is thick with weed on the edges. I thrash around desperately, calling her name. I wake just as my hand grasps her arm. I wish I hadn't. I don't know if I got to her in time.

☆     ☆

The main difficulty *is* having no one to share the responsibility. When things go wrong now, I can blame only myself. It is not a comforting thought, especially when you always expect disaster.

'How are your remarkably well-balanced children?' Shirley enquires on the telephone. It brings me to an abrupt stop. Well-balanced? It is hardly a term I would have used to describe them. Are they? Am I still expecting too much, failing to see the good, even when it is there under my nose? I do a quick mental inventory.

Margaret. I don't think I really believe what is happening to Margaret. After years of being overshadowed by two extremely powerful personalities she is beginning to emerge with distinct tastes and interests of her own, even if they do incline towards the punk. I hadn't thought about it before but that must surely rate as another miracle.

Then there's Deb, still fighting on all fronts, swinging from the mature to the immature, the sparkly to the impossible. 'Cute and lovable' the boys call her. She is, too, with her big brown eyes, warm personality, and a curly perm that cost a small fortune.

And David, my odd-job man? He has his heart set on studying architecture, 'anywhere but in London' he informs me. So that he can get away from the women, or this particular woman, anyway. It's a good job I know he is only indulging in that favourite male pastime of winding up the opposite sex, parent variety in particular. He is right. He must go. But we shall miss him. No one to chase Debra with snails, accompany Margaret to pop concerts, threaten to put Jenny fully clothed in the bath? Life won't be the same.

Kevin is talking one mealtime about David going to university.

'Yes, and what will we do then?' I say, indicating the little miss who appears absorbed in seeing how much mousse she can get on her nose, en route to her mouth.

Jenny looks up. 'That's OK,' she says placidly. 'When David's gone, we can have a cat.'

We laugh at the time, but it's not really a laughing matter. David is the only male who still occupies an important, everyday role in her life. She needs his toughness, his teasing, even if he does start to sneeze and come out in blotches when he has to share the same room as a cat.

Not to worry. There is always the holidays. I must stop rushing head-on to meet disasters months before we get to them. Come back to the here and now, Wendy. Concentrate on the pressing problems. Jenny starts at infant school after the Easter break. What am I going to do about their reading-scheme? It concentrates on building up simple sentences within the child's experience. I love my mum. I love my dad. My mum is pretty. My dad is big. How do we get round that one?

I resurrect an old folder of words, and a half-used exercise book. Jenny is delighted to be playing a new game, especially one with words. She makes sentences about David, Margaret, Debra, the dog, me. Draws pictures of punks, curly perms, David freckled like a giraffe. She turns a page. Who next? Pause. What shall we put for daddy?

She settles for 'My dad is dead. I am sad,' and draws a multi-coloured butterfly. It won't erase the ache of loss when the other children are talking about their fathers, but hopefully it will have given her some idea of how to handle the situation.

☆     ☆

'We haven't got another daddy yet, have we,' she announces, starting the day with the usual bang, as she and Snoopy arrive to prise me out of bed.

'No,' I grunt, trying to huddle further under the continental quilt.

'It's sad our daddy died, isn't it,' she continues undaunted, pulling the covers back, and climbing in beside me.

'Yes,' I sigh, surfacing reluctantly, without my much-needed transition from dreamland-to daydream-to harsh reality. 'We all miss him. But it's a year ago now, and God has looked after us. There have been lots of good things, too.'

She digests the idea slowly. The next 'Yes, but' has not quite had time to formulate. Strange how closely her reactions have paralleled my own. Relief, restlessness, yearning. Shirley reckons it is most unusual for a child so young to go through the normal stages of mourning. I wonder? Maybe she is just more able to articulate what she feels.

I wish I understood more of what the older ones feel. It's only occasionally their shutters fly back. Like Margaret, when Kevin wanted to borrow her camera: 'OK, but my dad bought it me, and if you lose it I'll never forgive you.' Or David, browsing through the photograph album. He pauses over some pictures of Jenny at eighteen months, flat on her stomach making mud pies amongst the daffodils.

'I remember dad taking those,' he says. 'They're my favourites.'

Deb is more open. And more vulnerable. I still don't

think I fully appreciate how badly all this must have hit her. The trouble is, she looks so mature. I've been classifying her as a 'teenager' for a couple of years at least, and most people think she's fifteen or sixteen. She sounds it, too, when she's acting as an Advice Columnist — telling me how to organize my life, stand up more for myself. Her current exasperation is my present crusade to solve the problems of the older generation.

'Why do you have to disrupt everything, when things are getting so much better?' she complains.

Sorry Deb, but you wait till you're caught in the middle of half a dozen different demands, trying to sort out the most pressing priorities. I have to remember that you children must come first, though; that the people you will become depends so much on me, just as little Jen reflects how we handle, or mishandle, her.

Thank you, God, for giving me another clue to her appalling behaviour at the mealtable. Her comment about missing daddy coming home each night. It all fits. End of children's programmes. Tea. The garage door grinding open, a bustle of books, papers, jackets, hugs. Daddy's home. For half a precious hour we are together as a family.

'Oh, God, if a forty-year-old can only function because Kevin is there to make six around the table, what must it be like for a four-year-old?'

It might not be so bad if all the good things didn't get submerged in the daily disputes over whose turn it is to do the washing-up, why someone has three chips fewer than the next person, and whether it really is essential to switch on the radio to pop music the minute you set foot in a room. And that's not to mention those who return from a pop concert at 2 a.m., and have forgotten their key; or who write their name on the lounge wall in red felt-tip, and then try to blame the dog; or who go to school with eight finger-nails painted red, and the thumb-nails spotted to look like a ladybird; or who collect seventeen lates, two disruptives, and a batch of answering-backs on their term's report.

It's then I need you, Pete. My wisdom, or lack of it, is not always sufficient. Two are stronger than one. Mind you, I'm not sure how you'd be coping in a house that sometimes feels more like an unattached youth club judging by the endless coffee cups, sprawling bodies, and never-ending music.

A friend came to dinner the other day and the three big ones put on their usual cabaret; non-stop verbal banter for a couple of hours. As she left, she remarked that it 'explained a lot'. The trouble was, she didn't say what it explained. Was it why I function at the intellectual level of an eighteen-year-old? How I've survived the last year? Or why I'm back on tranquillizers?

She tried to get out of it afterwards by saying it was just that she couldn't stand the pace. At least she now knows why I need to retreat occasionally; why I get so desperate for adult companionship.

You're great, kids. Really. I do love you. All of you. Especially from a safe distance.

☆     ☆

Another of my friends is dying. She knows it. Her husband knows. Their main concern is the children. They want to know what has helped ours to cope.

I ask them.

Was it having the situation explained? Being able to talk about Pete? Not having to camouflage their emotions?

'All those things,' says Margaret. 'But especially being told. We would have wondered anyway.'

'Not having to pretend,' Deb replies. 'If I felt bad about it I could cry, or say, 'cause I could see others doing it.'

David is at work. Jen I don't need to ask. I get told. Frequently.

'Why do we call the tree at the bottom of the garden daddy's tree?' she asks.

I explain how I used to look at it, and think about daddy, when he was ill in hospital. She studies the tree.

'It still puzzles me why daddy had to die,' she says.

Me too, Jen. I guess it always will.

☆     ☆

The shops are full of Easter eggs. I see only a shiny, golden one; remember your hope of the resurrection; curl up inside.

I try to find granny and grandad an Easter card. They are all of flowers and rabbits. Nothing to do with the Easter I know. That is about pain and darkness, a love which is tough and enduring. Gentle Jesus grown up to maturity, eyes wide open, fully aware of the cost. And paying it, so that his followers need never again be bound by sin, or fear, or death. The triumph of the human spirit, obedient to God's calling.

Like yours, Pete. Oh, love. It's OK for you. You've won your victory. I'm back in the thick of the battle, re-living your struggles. The iris and tulips are in flower in the front garden. Your tree is unfurling in the back. Wherever I turn I am confronted by memories, images of those last weeks. The hymns, sermons, are all to do with death and resurrection. They speak of triumph but only remind me of separation and loss. It is as much as I can do not to throw the hymnbook at the minister.

I wear dark clothes on a Sunday so that the tear stains are less obvious if I cannot smuggle my handkerchief out in time. I go to evening service and have to walk the streets for half an hour afterwards before I am calm enough to return to the demands of the family. The buds on the trees promise new life, new beginnings. I want the old back.

The lads in the house next door climb up your tree, and begin to lop off the branches. Jenny and I look at one another with terror in our eyes. There is nothing we can do to stop them. It is in their garden. But whatever will we do if they chop it down?

☆    ☆

Jenny is in the bath. She is playing with an assortment of beakers, funnels, squeezy bottles, strainers, happily absorbed for five minutes. Or so I think. She frowns as she concentrates on pouring water from one vessel to another.

'Daddy won't ever come back, will he?' she says.

I shake my head. 'No. He won't come back.'

It's still hard to believe. Even after a year. Which is why I'm running so hard from the reminders. Unlike Jenny, I still don't really want to acknowledge that fact.

☆    ☆

It is Easter Day. Joy. Hope. Celebration. You have to be joking. Come on, let's get it over. Dispense with the words and rituals as quickly as possible. Retreat. Take a picnic lunch into Epping Forest. Unwind a little. Erase the images. Laugh at the dog doing a belly flop in a patch of mud, the big ones playing pooh sticks in a winding stream. Kick my anger out on the carpet of beech leaves.

It is healing, calming, and oh, how I need it. I am running so fast, in ever-decreasing circles. Just one wrong word, and I would spin into the vortex, lost in the black hole of an empty self.

☆    ☆

We have booked a trip to Paris. In ten days' time it will be *the* anniversary. We need to occupy our minds and feet. It will be some small substitute for that cancelled holiday last year, and a good way of using the money donated by Peter's colleagues. Hopefully they will appreciate that time and memories can be more important than material goods.

Jan, my college friend, comes with us. You can see she is a teacher. At every stop she is counting heads, bags, tickets, kicking David into some kind of apology when he starts his Peter Sellers French impressions two minutes after setting foot on foreign soil.

I am not complaining. It is such a relief to have another adult willing to share the responsibility. Adult conversation. After a year of undiluted teenagers I feel as if I know more about the top twenty than ever before in my life, but precious little about anything else. By the time we have crossed the channel I feel a different person. The sea breezes have done nothing for the ache in my jaw, but already the one in my heart is easing.

☆    ☆

Paris is a delight, our hotel less impressive. A central

wooden staircase spirals up to our fifth-floor rooms. It appears to be the sole means of exit. The fire regulations would give a fire officer back home apoplexy. Roughly translated they read, 'In the event of a fire shut the door, block up any air holes, soak the door with water, stand by a window and make your presence known.' Seeing that our rooms overlook a charming, but apparently enclosed, central courtyard, quite what purpose that would serve is difficult to imagine, other than for waving happily at the folk on the opposite balcony.

Having an attractive teenage daughter is another hazard in a city where male sexuality is so blatantly flaunted. Judging by the car screeching to a halt in the middle of a bridge over the Seine, the number of eyes doing a quick strip on the metro, and the middle-aged man who nearly dislocated his neck at the click of her heels, women's lib. still has its bastilles to storm.

Margaret takes it all in her stride, *and* rescues me from two child pickpockets at the Arc de Triomphe.

Deb gets her own back when we go for a trip on the Seine. The embankment is littered with bodies making the most of the early heatwave. I doubt she could identify any of the buildings the guide is describing in four languages — she is too busy trying to make out if the men are wearing the briefest of swimming-trunks, or nothing at all.

David has his moment of glory in a very French restaurant. A French phrase book, dictionary and three-and-a-half French 'O' levels are little help in translating the menu, or ordering. He, like the rest of the diners, seems to think it all highly amusing. I rap him over the knuckles to bring him to order. Janet is scandalized.

'You shouldn't do that,' she rebukes me. 'In France children are precious.'

The waiter seems to think differently.

'You must do what your maman tells you,' he reproves David, tucking his serviette in like a bib. He obviously thinks I am telling him off for taking so long to eat his soup. In actual fact he has eaten his own and Margaret's, doing a quick change of bowls when the waiter's back was turned.

Deb laps it all up: food, coke, laughter, dishy black waiter.

'Can we come back here tomorrow?' she asks in a loud whisper.

I don't know that they'd have us, Deb. I can't think who you all take after.

☆    ☆

Notre Dame, the Pompidou centre, Sacré Coeur, the Louvre. They all get a look in, but I chicken out at the Eiffel Tower. I do not have a head for heights. Besides, I went up many lifetimes ago, on a school trip. I will enjoy being miserable sitting beneath the cherry blossom, reading the story of Heloise and Abelard, two star-crossed lovers of the twelfth century.

Janet shrugs her shoulders acceptingly. She didn't share a year with me at college for nothing. I obviously haven't changed.

Left to my own resources, and the tear-jerking conflicts others have experienced, I soon lapse into thought. You and me, Pete. In this city. Nine years ago. Our tenth wedding anniversary treat. We haven't moved at as rapid a pace as you spun me round the public transport system but we've gone fast enough to keep most of the memories at bay — until now. It was a mistake to sit still.

A group of youngsters straggle along the path, full of life, vitality, fun. There is something wholesome about their relationships in this city where so many are misused, distorted.

I find my tears turning to praise for the brief glimpses of goodness we see in your world, God, praying for more images to give us light in our own personal battles against the dark.

☆    ☆

On our last evening we make a special pilgrimage to see one of Peter's ex-staff who is living in the suburbs of Paris. After her own share of traumas she now has two delightful children, and a baby a few days old.

We talk, eat, drink, reminisce, admire the baby. Her

farewell hug comes from the depth of understanding the loss and loneliness of a broken relationship, and her own love and respect for Pete.

The wheel has come full circle. Last Easter she and the family spent half a day in London with us. They bought Peter a prayer plant. It was the only one of all the plants he was given to survive. I hope she understands that her prayers were answered, that death is not the defeat the deceiver would have us believe, for all the emptiness felt by those who are left behind.

☆　　☆

We are back home. I am restless. There is still another week to go.

'Don't be stupid like a horse or mule, which must be controlled with a bit and bridle to make it obey you,' warn the words from Psalms on the back of my wardrobe door.

I toss my head in defiance, then see the funny side of my reactions. It is a very apt description. I am exactly like an unschooled horse, tossing and bridling, on the end of the leading-rein. Left to my own devices I would soon break the restraints, and go careering off after anything and everything that might satiate this restlessness.

'I need those reins, God — your hand soothing, gentling, reassuring. Your voice reminding me, "Calm down. I'm here. It's going to be all right." '

I share the image with a friend.

'I've always thought of you as highly strung,' she says. 'Like a young colt.'

Another illusion shattered for ever. Whatever happened to the cool, calm, collected person she was supposed to see?

Ah well, hopefully it is just another 'phase'. Inevitable really, when you think about it. There are so many images to suppress, so many painful reminders of what was happening twelve months ago. I bury myself in my work, books, the children, people, plans for the future. One trick of the light, a voice, a story in a newspaper, and I am back with Peter, re-living his battles.

Poor Pete. You did your share of bucking and rearing

too, didn't you? But God won in the end. He led you into green pastures, beside the still waters. He restored your soul, so that when you went through the valley of shadows and out into the bright sunlight he was so close I almost envied you.

'There, I'm leaking again, God. You see? It still hurts. If the final stage is that of acceptance, I'm not there yet. Not by a long chalk.'

Someone said the other night, 'It doesn't get any easier. You just learn to live with it.'

I think she was right. But learn is the operative word. It takes time. It's a continuing process. The trouble is, you expect to be 'getting better'. Other people expect it of you. But so many things keep knocking you back. Sometimes I feel like one of those round-bottomed plastic 'kelly' dolls that we had when I was a child. You could hit them as hard as you liked but they would still bounce back upright. I envy them. I find it much harder to regain my equilibrium. It seems I usually just about manage it in time for the next blow.

Still, I was warned. Everyone said the first anniversary would be tough. I guess we survived last year because we were so relieved you were safe, Pete. No more sorrow. No more pain. Only for those left behind. Have I really survived nearly 365 days without you? It doesn't seem possible. Your tree is in full leaf again. The lads must have decided that chopping it down was too big a task. Mercifully. There are tassels of lime-green flowers, too. Soon, I suppose, they will turn into seeds. Helicopters. They will come twirling down into the garden. Next year there will be dozens of seedlings that I shall have to weed out, and the dog will promptly bring back to me. Not that you would really want to know. Never were one for gardening, were you? Always reckoned it would bring on an attack of hay fever, even in the middle of winter. Still, it helps to be aware of the cycle, to know that there is some kind of plan, purpose. Even if I can't see it, and it often seems hard to believe. Just as it seems hard to believe that this restlessness will pass, that one day life may return to some form of normality.

'I'm back on Psalms, God. You knew what you were doing when you harnessed the restless spirits of Old Testament times, didn't you? Understood that right through the centuries men and women would identify with their conflicts, their need of consolation and control. The world may have changed fairly drastically. Human nature remains pretty constant. We still need to pray a morning prayer for help.

"You give me victory and restore my courage,
I call to the Lord for help . . . and he answers me."

'Thank you, God, that I haven't had to pretend. You understand my turmoil of emotions, know why I go leaping and cavorting around the place. Thank you even more for the confidence that comes from knowing that your hands are firm on the ends of the reins. You hold me. And you won't let go.'

# POSTSCRIPT

Well . . . we have made it. The first year is over, but I have run so hard I am exhausted. I know my limits, and I am very near the edge. If I don't calm down I will be joining Peter sooner than any of us expected. Someone suggests a weekend conference in the country in June. I clutch it with both hands. No children? No duties? No demands? Something to stretch my mind? They don't need to ask twice. It will do me more good than any of the doctors' remedies.

A play about St Francis helps towards the healing. Apparently he too found difficulty in learning to walk in God's space, God's time. There's hope for the rest of us yet, then. I needed that reminder. I've spent so much of the past year sorting things out in my time, my terms. Mind you, I make no apology. I think it had to be. No one else could do it for me.

'Now you're tugging the reins a little tighter, God, letting me know who's boss. Fair enough. I'm not complaining. Without your discipline and love I dread to think where we might have ended.'

Ended? That's a joke. There's a long, hard haul still ahead. I'm still stuck in the slow lane, but I think maybe the worst is past.

We lost someone we loved dearly. We needed to mourn. It is fitting. There is no other way. A woman who has spent many years advising people with relationship problems says that grief is the price we pay for loving.

'She is right, isn't she, God? You know that only too well. Yet still you go on loving, energizing, creating, renewing. So . . . where does that leave me?'

As if I didn't know. Someone sent me a postcard this morning. A simple, black-and-white illustration of a signpost: one arm labelled 'yesterday', the other 'tomorrow'. The person who sent it did not even realize the possible implications until it was too late. But the timing was impeccable. I needed that jolt.

I am faced with a choice. I can stay living in the past,

some part of me buried with Peter. Or I can move forward, taking the part of him that will always be with me and the children, on into the future.

I know there will be lapses, times when the past will overtake, overwhelm me. It did yesterday. One of Jenny's gerbils died, and its mate was running round the cage looking for it. When I burst into tears I knew it wasn't really the gerbil I was crying for.

'But your calling is always onward, forward, no matter how many times we stumble, or stage a sit-down protest. There is really only one choice of direction for those who put their trust in you, isn't there? So be it. Even if the way ahead is still strewn with boulders, you have kept your promises. There is no reason to doubt that some day we, too, will come out into bright sunlight.'